REDEEMED

OUR LIVES AS SINNERS AND SAINTS

DAN HOPPEN

CONCORDIA PUBLISHING HOUSE • SAINT LOUIS

Published by Concordia Publishing House
3558 S. Jefferson Avenue, St. Louis, MO 63118-3968
1-800-325-3040 • cph.org

Library of Congress Cataloging-in-Publication Data

Names: Hoppen, Dan

Title: Redeemed : our lives as sinners and saints / Dan Hoppen.
Description: Saint Louis, MO : Concordia Publishing House, [2021] |
Summary: "How many times have we heard the words "God loves you" and yet not believed them because we have made a wreck of our lives and felt unworthy of His love? We hear those words all the time, but how can we see them in action? We see them through God's power to redeem and repair broken lives. In Redeemed, adult Christians will find examples of God's redemption as they explore several key Bible characters who really messed things up. Readers will see how God forgave and restored these people, repaired the damage, and brought meaning and purpose in their lives. Though readers may feel that their failings have erected a permanent barrier between themselves and God, they will learn how God redeems His people time and time again-through the Word and Sacraments, their church, friends, family, and other circumstances"-- Provided by publisher.

Identifiers: LCCN 2021018142 (print) | LCCN 2021018143 (ebook) | ISBN 9780758669926 | ISBN 9780758669933 (ebook)
Subjects: LCSH: Redemption--Biblical teaching. | Sin--Biblical teaching. | Bible--Biography.
Classification: LCC BT775 .R35 2021 (print) | LCC BT775 (ebook) | DDC 234/.3--dc23
LC record available at https://lccn.loc.gov/2021018142
LC ebook record available at https://lccn.loc.gov/2021018143

Manufactured in the United States of America

---

1 2 3 4 5 6 7 8 9 10   30 29 28 27 26 25 24 23 22 21

Scripture. Grace. Truth. Transformation.
Once again, Dan Hoppen brings the Word of God and love of Jesus to life through his whimsical and exquisite writing. This book is a novel, Bible study, must-read, and must-share all in one. Each page, illustration, and application is identifiable and applicable to our lives today. Dan illustrates the truth of the Scriptures as living and active, sharper than any double-edged sword. I can't wait to see how God uses this book for the encouragement and growth of the Kingdom through the Holy Spirit.

Rev. Greg S. Griffith, lead pastor, King of Kings, Omaha, NE

Too often, the beloved heroes of the Bible are exalted to a saintly standard one should emulate. Yet this task is dangerously self-defeating when Christians ponder the depths of their own sin. Author Dan Hoppen pulls down these impossible ideals from their respective pedestals. His conversational style and humorous pop-culture whit make seemingly unrelatable figures more relatable to contemporary readers. *Redeemed* explores how Christ used these figures despite their failings, as opposed to through their greatness. Similarly, Jesus—the Redeemer—can salvage each of us, no matter how far we feel we've fallen down the pit of sin.

Rev. Eric T. Eichinger, senior pastor, Bethel Lutheran Church, Clearwater, FL
Author of *The Final Race* and *Lord of Legends: Jesus' Redemption Quest*

Life is messy and getting messier. The pitfalls and rabbit holes that sin can lead the Christian down are many. This book is built around the tension that exists in every Christian's life—living as a sinner who, through the cleansing blood of Jesus, is made a saint. Author Dan Hoppen walks the reader through fourteen easily identifiable, highly relatable sin trails while bringing the reader to the only place of consolation—the cross. Every reader will be confronted with a moment of deep introspection and application. This is a tremendous resource for the individual who is willing to let down their guard, search their heart, and allow the Word of God to bring peace and forgiveness to their messy world!

Rev. Dr. Jeffrey E. Skopak, senior pastor, Grace Lutheran Church and School, Jacksonville, FL

This book is for Christians who struggle with sin and are loved by Jesus. Dan Hoppen explores the contours of justification and sanctification as each chapter meditates on a moment in the life of God's people, who fail and yet are redeemed. For Christians who know the struggle of sin, even after Baptism, this book speaks an apt word of love and grace.

Rev. Jacob Schultz, pastor, Concordia Lutheran Church, Kirkwood, MO

In your hands is a book of hope. Dan Hoppen here provides a biblically rich and thoroughly practical guidebook for life as a Christian. It's a book that points us to God's steadfast love for us in Jesus Christ, a message that provides a sense of grounding and certainty in an uncertain and changing world. You'll benefit from Hoppen's insights, you'll be comforted by the assurance that you are not alone in your struggles, and you'll be led to our ultimate hope—Jesus Christ.

Rev. Brian Davies, pastor, Lord of Glory Lutheran Church, Grayslake, IL
Author of *Connected to Christ: Overcoming Isolation through Community*

Table of Contents

PREFACE

"Benny, come!"

At the sound of my voice, a fuzzy head emerged from the grove of hosta plants in our backyard, and a pair of inquisitive eyes studied me from afar.

It was November 2020; three weeks prior, my wife, Sarah, and I had just adopted our first pet together. Our Golden Retriever puppy was adorable, healthy, and—for the most part—extremely well-behaved. Benny was also an incredibly quick learner, which is what made moments such as this one so frustrating.

I was working from home at the time, which allowed me to take Benny outside for quick breaks to relieve himself and burn off some energy. But I had been out with him for about ten minutes now, and I needed to get back to work. It was time to come inside.

"Benny, come!"

Our eyes locked, and I could feel Benny evaluating me. At this point, he knew the meaning of *come*, and he was well aware that obeying this command not only resulted in love and exclamations of "Good boy!" but often a treat as well. If he obeyed, he'd be rewarded.

Yet after about a three-second staring contest, Benny turned and romped in the other direction, far more interested in exploring the yard than coming inside.

He deliberately disobeyed me. Cute as he was bounding after the rustling leaves, my blood boiled inside. I grabbed him and brought him inside to the kitchen, where Sarah was working on dinner.

"I just don't get it," I groused. "He knows exactly what I want him to do. He's obeyed in the past. Why does he defy me to do his own thing, especially when I have a treat waiting for him?"

Before Sarah could even answer, I was floored by the foolishness of my complaint.

Because I'm Benny, and so are you.

No, we're not a fluffy ten-week-old puppy with eyes soft enough to melt Ebenezer Scrooge's heart. But we are rebels without a cause, senselessly defying our Master, who has nothing but our best interests at heart: God.

How many times do you feel the pull of temptation, knowing that following through on that desire is wrong? Maybe it's a tug to cheat or lie to get ahead at work. Or you give into human desires through pornography or a sexual relationship outside of marriage. Perhaps you know chasing the bottle isn't the right way to respond to a rough day, but you find yourself pouring a third glass of whiskey.

I'll admit it; I disobey all the time, even as I acknowledge that if Jesus were standing next to me, I definitely wouldn't engage in that activity. (Of course, He is with me at all times.) God's commandments are clearly spelled out for us, and He also gave us the Holy Spirit (Galatians 5:16–21) to help us stay on the right path.

Yet when He calls for us, we run away from Him, so distracted by the fleeting pleasures of our current situation that we fail to see the long-term benefits of sprinting to our loving God.

Here's the good news: your favorite biblical hero is Benny too.

That's right: the pillars of our faith—Moses, David, Peter, Paul, the whole gang—all ran away from God. As faith-filled and inspirational as these people were, they lost their way at times too, and yet God didn't abandon them. He empowered them to do incredible things and change the world.

The good news, dear reader, is that no matter how many times you've turned away from God or how many times you have sinned, He loves you.

The skeptic reads that sentence like a Sunday School message. *Jesus loves you, no matter what.* Christianity is all rainbows and unicorns, right?

(It's not, by the way. Just check John 16:33.)

The skeptic wants proof. Words are cheap and empty; action is confirmation.

That's what this book is for. It examines biblical characters who committed sins I'm willing to bet you can very easily relate to, such as pride, doubt, rebelliousness, and lukewarm living. We'll zoom in on why these inspirational people chose to stray from the path they knew was right.

But more importantly, we'll look at how God responded to them.

That's the awesome thing about the Bible—if you want proof of God's goodness, the pages overflow with it. Humans, even those we hold up as standards of our faith, constantly screw up. That's the reality of sin. Romans 3:23 tells us, "For all have sinned and fall short of the glory of God."

Our sin has earned us an eternity of suffering in hell. But through Jesus' sacrifice, God created another way (John 3:16–17).

Because of God's great mercy, we are no longer under the sentence of damnation, but we can enjoy eternal paradise with our Father in heaven!

Still skeptical? Open the Bible.

We'll look at fourteen particular shortcomings human beings typically encounter, and we'll use real-life examples to see how God responded:

- Gideon was a prophet who doubted God and constantly needed reminders and signs that God would come through for him.
- David was an adulterer who chased the pleasures of the flesh over what he knew was right.
- Jonah was a vengeful fugitive who defied God's order.
- Peter routinely gave into fear despite his confession being described by Jesus as the rock upon which He would build His Church (Matthew 16:18).

And on and on and on. Pick a sin, any sin; one of your favorite biblical characters committed it.

And yet, God didn't condemn them. He loved them.

In addition, each chapter will take a look at how Jesus responded when put in a similar situation. He was human, and He was tempted. Yet He never sinned. That's why He could be our substitute and our Savior. What can we learn from His actions to inspire our own?

"Benny, come!"

As he matured from puppy to dog, Benny's mistakes became few and far between. He realized that obeying had positive results, while resisting our commands brought negative consequences.

He was never perfect, but he continued to improve and desired to please his masters.

So it is with us and God. As we understand and honor the incredible things He has done for us, we have no choice but to respond with thankfulness and love. This doesn't mean we'll be perfect—far from it—but His great mercy causes us to aspire to be better, to lift our heads from the hostas and come bounding to our Father, who's waiting with far more than a treat in His hand.

Want proof? Let's dig in.

CHAPTER 1

Broken Relationships

If possible, so far as it depends
on you, live peaceably with all.
(Romans 12:18)

If Shaq and Kobe had wanted to, they could have ruled the NBA.

For a short time, that's exactly what they did. From 2000 to 2002, the Los Angeles Lakers won 74 percent of their games and took home three straight NBA titles. At the center of it all was Shaquille O'Neal, the overwhelming beast of a center who was nearly unstoppable in the low post, and Kobe Bryant, the lithe, athletic guard with a smooth handle and a killer edge. On paper, the two perfectly complemented each other. It seemed they were destined to dominate the league for the foreseeable future.

Despite all their success, a fissure developed between the Lakers' superstars. Both Shaq and Kobe had alpha-dog personalities. They each wanted to be on top, and each bristled when his costar received more of the credit. Over time, a great resentment grew between them. They sniped at each other in the press and bickered on and off the court.

Their feud came to a head when the Lakers were upset by the underdog Detroit Pistons in the 2004 Finals. At that point, the Lakers had no choice but to split up Kobe and Shaq, and they traded O'Neal to the Miami Heat.

As talented as both were and as well as they fit together, Kobe and Shaq allowed minor squabbles to come between them, and they butted heads until they were forced to go their separate ways. NBA historians still debate how many titles the pair could have brought home had they been able to leave their egos aside and find harmony.

Sometimes I wonder if that's how God felt about Paul and Barnabas.

Barnabas

Paul and Barnabas were a tag-team duo that put the Lakers to shame. They took the biblical landscape by storm, starting churches and creating new believers all across the Middle East.

As it turned out, the only thing that could stop these two was themselves.

As the author of thirteen books in the Bible, Paul is one of the most important figures in the New Testament. The way he boldly proclaimed the Gospel after Jesus appeared to him on the road to Damascus played a huge role in keeping the faith alive despite severe persecution from the Jewish leaders.

Without Barnabas, however, Paul's ministry might have fallen flat from the get-go. Remember, when we first read about Paul, he was Saul, the Christian-hunting menace who wanted to squash Christianity. He switched course after encountering Christ on the road to Damascus (Acts 9:1–19), but the early Christians were understandably wary of his newfound faith. Saul had been a merciless villain, and the people believed this "new Saul" was only a ploy to win their trust and entrap them (Acts 9:26).

Can you blame them? Saul was the same man who casually looked on as Stephen was stoned in the street (Acts 7:57–60). He caused havoc for the Church, entering every house, dragging off men and women, and committing them to prison (Acts 9:1–2).

His very threat caused the Christians to scatter all over the region, and Saul continued to pursue them doggedly.

There was no greater enemy than Saul to the Early Christian Church. And now the Christians were expected to believe this menace had turned over a new leaf?

Put it this way: if you see an angry grizzly bear charging at you, are you going to try and give it a hug? Or will you run like mad in the opposite direction?

The believers weren't going to trust Saul unless one of their leaders vouched for him; given Saul's track record, that appeared to be a very dangerous proposition.

Barnabas stepped in on Saul's behalf. He had established a sterling reputation among the believers, and he had heard how Saul had changed and boldly preached about Jesus in Damascus. Barnabas stepped out in faith and embraced the newcomer, and his stamp of approval helped the believers accept Saul (Acts 9:27).

Immediately, the Christians' attitudes toward Saul were tested. He joined the apostles and began boldly preaching around Jerusalem, a move that didn't sit well with his former employers. When he got into a heated debate with some Greek-speaking Jews, they decided his conversion was worthy of a death sentence. But when the believers heard about the murderous plot, they rescued him and helped him escape to his home in Tarsus (Acts 9:28–30).

In a short time, the Christians went from fearing and despising Saul to saving his life. Such was the influence that Barnabas's words held.

Barnabas was a very effective teacher on his own (Acts 11:23–24), but he really believed in Saul. As Barnabas established the Church in Antioch (Acts 11:19–21), he decided Saul would be the perfect partner. Barnabas went to Tarsus and brought Saul back to Antioch. The duo stayed there for a year and converted so many people that Antioch became the birthplace of the term *Christians* (Acts 11:26).

From there, the Holy Spirit sent them to Cyprus, Antioch of Pisidia, Iconium, Lystra, and Derbe before returning them to Antioch of Syria. They showed Christ's love to the Gentiles (Acts 13:26, 46–49; 14:1), filled newfound believers with the Holy Spirit (Acts 13:52), and performed miraculous signs and healings through God's power (Acts 14:3, 8–10). They shamed stuck-up Jewish leaders (Acts 13:50–51), escaped death threats (Acts 14:5–6), and preached so boldly that some thought they were gods, though they quickly and humbly shot down that notion (Acts 14:11–18).

Powered by the Holy Spirit, Paul and Barnabas were an impenetrable tank steamrolling over any situation the devil put in their path. In fact, Paul was at one point stoned by the Jews, dragged outside Lystra, and left for dead. A short time later, this apparently dead man got up and went back into town. Can you imagine the double takes he got walking around the very streets where he was supposedly killed the previous day?

This two-man wrecking crew couldn't be stopped. Threaten them, insult them, bludgeon them within an inch of their life; it didn't matter. They just kept coming, preaching boldly about Jesus and broadcasting His truth to more and more people, both Jews and Gentiles.

At the end of their missionary journey, Paul and Barnabas returned to Antioch, where they stayed for some time with the believers there. Their first trip had been a rousing success, but it appeared to be just the tip of the iceberg. There was no ceiling on what these two could do for Christ together.

Then came the issue of John Mark.

John Mark, Barnabas's cousin, was clearly a man with great spiritual passion. The eventual author of the Gospel of Mark, he was picked by Paul and Barnabas to join them on their first missionary journey. This was no random selection or act of nepotism on Barnabas's part; Paul and Barnabas knew this journey would be long, challenging, and dangerous, and they needed a spiritual warrior by their side. By selecting John Mark as their assistant (Acts 12:25; 13:5), Paul and Barnabas put their stamp of approval on him.

It turned out to be a short-term decision.

We aren't told why, but John Mark bailed early in the journey. Perhaps he was homesick, or he underestimated the dangers and rigors of the journey. Maybe he only planned on going so far and failed to communicate this properly to his traveling companions. We can speculate on his departure all day long, but we only get two hard facts out of the story:

- When the group sailed to Perga in Pamphylia, John Mark left them to return to Jerusalem (Acts 13:13).
- His desertion shattered Paul's confidence in him (Acts 15:38).

Undeterred by John Mark's exit, Paul and Barnabas pressed on and accomplished all kinds of great things for God before returning to Antioch of Syria.

After some time, Paul approached Barnabas about a return tour to check on how the new believers were doing and to encourage their young faith. Barnabas was all in, but he wanted to bring John Mark along too.

That was a deal-breaker for Paul, who was still deeply hurt by John Mark's desertion.

I can understand the thought processes of both men here:

- **Paul:** You seriously want to bring John Mark with us? He already deserted us once, and he's done nothing to earn our trust. Besides, we're better off on our own. If you really think we need additional companions, Silas (Acts 15:40) or Timothy (Acts 16:1–3) would be far better candidates.
- **Barnabas:** John Mark is my relative, and I stand by him. Yes, he messed up before. But I believe in him and his ability to help us. And who are you, Paul, to say that people can't have a dramatic turnaround? Give John Mark a second chance.

The line was drawn in the sand. Neither man was going to budge.

A "sharp disagreement" arose (Acts 15:36–40), and tensions escalated to the point that both men concluded it would be better if they parted ways. Barnabas and John Mark went to Cyprus, while Paul chose Silas to accompany him throughout Syria and Cilicia. As far as we know, Barnabas and Paul never saw each other again.

Their story makes Shaq and Kobe's spat seem like an amicable breakup.

I can't help but read this account and wonder how such a minor issue could break this sturdy bond. These two traveled hundreds of miles over several years. Together, they had changed lives, performed miracles, faced death threats, and opened God's love to the Gentiles. Think of all the meals they shared, all the laughs around the campfire, all the heart-to-heart discussions as they walked along the roads between destinations.

These men were more than friends; they were brothers (Proverbs 17:17). For a great while, Paul and Barnabas personified Romans 12:10: "Love one another with brotherly affection. Outdo one another in showing honor."

Somehow, that connection was torn to pieces in one conversation.

Their split shows what can happen when we allow minor rifts to grow into major problems. Instead of looking for a compromise, both men stubbornly dug in their heels and refused to budge. Paul and Barnabas allowed the devil to get his hooks into their relationship and tear them apart from the inside. A great tag team was sabotaged.

The Bible encourages us to pursue harmonious relationships with fellow Christians. Rather than squabble over minor issues, we're called to look for ways to consider one another's opinions and support one another:

> Finally, all of you, have unity of mind, sympathy, brotherly love, a tender heart, and a humble mind. (1 Peter 3:8)

> Live in harmony with one another. Do not be haughty, but associate with the lowly. Never be wise in your own sight. (Romans 12:16)

> I appeal to you, brothers, by the name of our Lord Jesus Christ, that all of you agree, and that there be no divisions among you, but that you be united in the same mind and the same judgment. (1 Corinthians 1:10)

Sympathetic. Humble. Perfectly united. All things that Paul and Barnabas were not.

Even these biblical titans allowed their pride to get in the way. Barnabas wouldn't budge in his selection of John Mark, although there were other worthy candidates to join him and Paul on their mission. Paul refused to admit that in the years since his abandonment, John Mark might have matured and was worthy of a second chance.

Much as I want to chastise Paul and Barnabas, their conflict brings to mind my freshman year of college and a similar falling out I had with my roommate.

When I arrived at Hastings College, I didn't know a soul. I had chosen the school for basketball, and for the first time in my life, I found myself separated from all my family and friends. As far as I could tell, there was one other person on the basketball team who felt like me: my roommate, Joe.

For the first few months, we were nearly inseparable. We ate together at the cafeteria, lifted in the weight room with each other, battled opponents on *Call of Duty*, and made frequent trips to visit our friends at the University of Nebraska in Lincoln. For a while, he was my best friend.

But over time, small cracks formed in our relationship. He would spend hours talking on the phone with his girlfriend, and their talks (and fights) would often last long into the night. We only had one television in our dorm room, and I could see his frustration every time he entered the room and I was using it. We never had a major disagreement like Paul and Barnabas, but we slowly grew to resent each other. I can probably count on one hand the number of times we spoke over our last two months as roommates; when I moved out, I didn't even bother saying goodbye.

It all seems so stupid in retrospect. I actively contributed to a hostile living situation, and for no reason. Maybe Joe and I weren't intended to be best friends forever, but rather than try to improve our relationship, I stubbornly dug in my heels and ignored him. I was proud, I was conceited, and I helped create a division between us—all things we're specifically called to avoid in the verses above.

Does this mean that you should cave and always agree with other people, whether you align with them or not? Absolutely not! God doesn't call you to be a pushover:

> Be watchful, stand firm in the faith, act like men, be strong. (1 Corinthians 16:13)

> Therefore, my beloved brothers, be steadfast, immovable, always abounding in the work of the Lord, knowing that in the Lord your labor is not in vain. (1 Corinthians 15:58)

> But in your hearts honor Christ the Lord as holy, always being prepared to make a defense to anyone who asks you for a reason for the hope that is in you; yet do it with gentleness and respect, having a good

> conscience, so that, when you are slandered, those who revile your good behavior in Christ may be put to shame. (1 Peter 3:15–16)

There are plenty of times when the right call is to steadfastly stand our ground. Your beliefs won't be in lockstep with everyone else's, and you have to determine if certain relationships are worth continuing. Pray about it; I'm willing to bet God will let you know which are important and which can be let go.

You can be confident in this: He'll make the best out of whatever choice you make.

Back to Paul and Barnabas.

I can picture the devil sneering and chuckling to himself as the two parted ways in a huff. The duo was a major threat, and he had managed to break them apart. This could be a crippling blow to the early Christian movement, the very thing he needed to erase the momentum Jesus and the Early Church had created.

But, as always, God saw the bigger picture.

God turned the breakup into a blessing. Paul's missionary success is well-documented, and Silas proved to be a perfect companion (witness his incredible faith in Acts 16:16–40). And John Mark, as Barnabas predicted, developed into a great warrior for the faith. Look at the way Paul, John Mark's greatest detractor, eventually referred to him:

> Luke alone is with me. Get Mark and bring him with you, for he is very useful to me for ministry. (2 Timothy 4:11)

> Aristarchus my fellow prisoner greets you, and Mark the cousin of Barnabas (concerning whom you have

> received instructions—if he comes to you, welcome him). (Colossians 4:10)

By splitting up His power players, God actually doubled the number of lives Barnabas and Paul were able to touch, and His move allowed John Mark, Silas, and Timothy (Philippians 2:20–22) to be developed along the way. The devil's supposed win was quickly transformed into a defeat.

God responded by turning dispute into victory, and He always holds the power to do so. But we're called to live in harmony with one another for a reason. We shouldn't always depend on God to save our relationships with powerful acts; rather, we need to try our best to approach one another with compassion and love, even when those around us do the unthinkable.

Joseph and His Ten Brothers

You think your siblings are bad?

I'm willing to bet they never considered killing you, sold you into slavery, or faked your death.

In fairness to Joseph's brothers, you probably also never told your siblings you had visions they would bow to you one day.

It's safe to say there was a bit of strife in Joseph's family. Relationships were strained to their breaking point, but because of love, they were able to be saved at the most critical moment.

Let's jump all the way back to Genesis 37, where we find that Jacob, now an old man, has settled in the land of Canaan. He had twelve sons, and he made no attempt to hide which was his favorite. Jacob lavished Joseph with a colorful, ornate robe, the kind usually reserved for royalty, as a sign of his affection.

That didn't sit well with the other boys, who "hated [Joseph] and could not speak peacefully to him" (Genesis 37:4).

Imagine a family that passes down an old car from kid to kid. This piece of junk has over 200,000 miles on it and is beat to pieces, but it just keeps kicking, so it remains in the family rotation. Then the youngest son turns sixteen, and Dad splurges by buying him a brand-new Lamborghini. That's going to ruffle some feathers, right?

Tensions were high and family peace rested on the edge of a machete—one wrong move and things were going to get ugly. Joseph ended up pushing the group over the edge.

Joseph had a prophetic dream from God in which he and his brothers were in the field tying bundles of grain. All at once, his bundle stood up, while his brothers' bundles gathered around and bowed low. The symbolism isn't hard to see here; God was showing Joseph that though he was younger, he would become the greatest of his family.

To receive such a message is an awesome blessing!

It's also maybe not one to share with people who already don't care for you.

This nuance was lost on Joseph. In his youthful brilliance, he chose not to keep this dream to himself. Instead, he bragged about it to everyone.

I'll give you one guess how that went over.

And yet, Joseph didn't learn his lesson. Soon after, he had a similar dream, and again he couldn't refrain from running his mouth. In his second dream, his father and mother were bowing to him as well. This proclamation earned him a rare scolding from his dad and essentially sealed his fate with his brothers. Whatever tatters of a relationship he'd had with them were torn to shreds.

Joseph's brothers catch most of the flak for ruining the family bond (if you're unfamiliar with this story, you're about to see why). But I think it's important to recognize that Joseph's self-glory was what cracked his brothers' patience. Call it whatever you like: youthful naivete, callous arrogance, whatever. When he received blessings, whether it was a colorful cloak from his father or predictive dreams from God, he flaunted them in front of his brothers. His boasts turned his brothers into jealous, murderous schemers.

That's how Joseph found himself in a terrible situation one day. The rest of his brothers were some distance away, tending to the family's flocks of sheep. Jacob sent Joseph out to check on them and get a progress report. When his brothers saw him coming from a distance, their minds immediately went to a dark place:

> Come now, let us kill him and throw him into one of the pits. Then we will say that a fierce animal has devoured him, and we will see what will become of his dreams. (Genesis 37:20)

Before we move on, I want you to think about the angriest you've ever been at someone. I'm willing to bet you had some pretty harsh thoughts about that person. Maybe you even wished them harm.

But I, for one, cannot even fathom the idea of hating someone so much that I would even remotely consider ending someone's life. The root of such thoughts is pure evil. I don't blame Joseph's brothers for disliking him. But to entertain killing him?

The Bible makes no bones about it; we are not ever to consider taking another life, regardless of the wrongs they have dealt us:

> Whoever takes a human life shall surely be put to death. (Leviticus 24:17)

> Whoever sheds the blood of man, by man shall his blood be shed, for God made man in His own image. (Genesis 9:6)

That's just obvious, right? It doesn't take a biblical scholar to tell you murder is wrong.

But we're also told that if we let hatred seep into our hearts, we grow closer to murder, even if we're not physically harming another:

> Everyone who hates his brother is a murderer, and you know that no murderer has eternal life abiding in him. (1 John 3:15)

> You have heard that it was said to those of old, "You shall not murder; and whoever murders will be liable to judgment." But I say to you that everyone who is angry with his brother will be liable to judgment; whoever insults his brother will be liable to the council; and whoever says, "You fool!" will be liable to the hell of fire. (Matthew 5:21–22)

Broken relationships go two ways. Yes, Joseph was a spoiled braggart who drove his older brothers crazy. But rather than let their anger subside or pray about it, they stored up hatred and were liable for God's judgment before they even vocalized their plans to end his life.

Fortunately, Jacob's eldest son Reuben saw through the bloodlust to realize the insanity of this discussion. He convinced the rest of them to throw Joseph into a nearby cistern (a large hole dug in the ground to store rainwater), where they would leave him to die and technically avoid having his blood on their hands.

Secretly, Reuben planned to return once emotions had cooled and rescue Joseph, but his half-measure backfired. While he was away (we're not told where or why), a caravan of Ishmaelite traders passed by, and the rest of the brothers decided they may as well make some money off Joseph. They sold him as a slave to the passersby, and Joseph was hauled off to Egypt in chains. Then the brothers soaked Joseph's precious robe in goat's blood and brought it back to Jacob, claiming Joseph had been killed by a wild animal.

Technically, they spared his life. But the brothers well knew that even if Joseph survived the hot trek through the desert, a life of misery awaited him. They had essentially signed his death warrant.

At this point, these relationships seem well beyond the point of reconciliation. Joseph had boastfully predicted that his family would bow to him, and his brothers retaliated by selling him as a slave. You can't find a soap opera dramatic enough to make this stuff up.

And yet, like a dandelion sprouting up through cracks of cement, a sliver of hope remained for the family. Joseph may have been a bit strong-headed, but he developed into a God-fearing man. When the time arrived for him to crush his family, he instead chose to resurrect seemingly dead relationships.

Were I to dive into the next thirteen years of Joseph's life in full detail, I'd make a J. R. R. Tolkien novel look like a haiku. Let's hit the highlights instead:

- Joseph was sold by the traders to the Egyptian officer Potiphar (Genesis 39:1).

- He impressed Potiphar so much that he was promoted to head of his household (Genesis 39:6).
- He was betrayed by Potiphar's promiscuous wife, whom he refused despite her numerous advances (Genesis 39:7–18).
- He was thrown into prison (Genesis 39:19–20).
- He was forgotten by the cup-bearer he had befriended in prison (Genesis 40).

Just know this: while Joseph's brothers may have left him for dead, God did the opposite. He had a glorious plan for His child, difficult as it was to see on the surface.

Joseph remained in Egyptian prison for years before his time for redemption arrived. Eventually, Pharaoh had two dreams that deeply disturbed him. He was certain they had meaning, so he called upon his magicians and wise men to interpret them. But when Pharaoh explained his visions, they couldn't tell him his dreams' meaning.

The king's cup-bearer had been with Joseph in prison for two years before Joseph interpreted the cup-bearer's dream that he would be restored to his former position. Finally, this man remembered he once had a friend who knew a thing or two about dreams (better late than never, I guess). When Joseph was summoned, he interpreted that Pharaoh's dreams meant the land would undergo seven years of great prosperity, followed by seven years of crippling famine. He advised Pharaoh to find a wise man who would oversee the storing of crops during the good years, giving Egypt plenty of stored food to eat when the famine arrived.

Pharaoh was so impressed that he gave Joseph the job on the spot.

> Then Pharaoh said to Joseph, "Since God has shown you all this, there is none so discerning and wise as you are. You shall be over my house, and all my people shall order themselves as you command. Only as regards the throne will I be greater than you." (Genesis 41:39–40)

From the dungeon to second-in-command of Egypt. Not a bad afternoon.

I think it's really important to recognize the juxtaposition between how Joseph approached dreams at this moment versus his approach in his youth. When he was a youngster, he boasted about the blessings God had shown him. In Pharaoh's court, he displayed incredible humility:

- Joseph answered Pharaoh, "It is not in me; God will give Pharaoh a favorable answer." (Genesis 41:16)
- "God has revealed to Pharaoh what He is about to do." (Genesis 41:25)
- "God has shown to Pharaoh what He is about to do." (Genesis 41:28)
- "The doubling of Pharaoh's dream means that the thing is fixed by God, and God will shortly bring it about." (Genesis 41:32)

Joseph developed some serious humility as he matured. While he had once lauded his dreams over his brothers, he now turned all ownership of his dream interpretation over to God. He had every opportunity to take credit for this miraculous ability for himself, but he chose to turn the spotlight back on God. He had learned from his mistakes.

Just as Joseph predicted, the next seven years were very fruitful, and Joseph gathered one-fifth of all the crops for storage. There was so much excess, he stopped keeping records.

Once the seven years ended, however, the second half of Joseph's prophecy came true. A crushing famine struck Egypt and the surrounding countries. When the people of Egypt cried out to Pharaoh for food, he sent them to Joseph, who opened his storehouses and distributed valuable grain to the Egyptians. Word of this stockpile spread, and soon people from surrounding lands were traveling to Egypt to buy grain from Joseph.

That included a certain family of shepherds in Canaan.

Jacob's family was in dire straits, so he sent his eldest ten sons to Egypt to buy grain. But he wouldn't allow his youngest, Benjamin, to go on the journey out of fear that something might happen to him. The brothers made the trek to Egypt and presented themselves before this food overlord who now held their future in his hands.

They had no idea this man was their brother, the child they had betrayed all those years ago.

They may not have recognized Joseph, who had matured and was now adorned in fancy Egyptian garb, but he definitely knew who they were. I cannot even imagine the knot that formed in Joseph's throat as his brothers "bowed themselves before him with their faces to the ground" (Genesis 42:6). They were his blood, but they had also sold him as a slave. That's a pretty complex set of emotions we're dealing with here.

Also, remember a certain dream from all those years ago, one involving bundles of grain? Joseph's brothers may not have liked it then, but Joseph's prophecy had now come true.

His feelings conflicted, Joseph didn't take action one way or the other. Instead, he offered a test.

He accused his brothers of being spies, upon which they revealed they had a younger brother who had remained back at their home with their father. Joseph placed them in prison for three days (okay, maybe he held a little bit of a grudge) before allowing the brothers to go and retrieve Benjamin, thus proving they weren't undercover agents from another land. But he kept one of them, Simeon, as a prisoner until the brothers returned with Benjamin.

On the surface, it doesn't seem like Joseph was trying to mend any fences by accusing his brothers of being spies, giving them a quick timeout in prison, and keeping Simeon. But these weren't purely vengeful acts on Joseph's part. He guessed Benjamin had assumed his role as Jacob's favorite, and now he had to know how the others treated him. Did they resent Benjamin as they had Joseph? Or had they learned from their mistake and matured?

By not taking revenge, Joseph left the door cracked. The relationship could survive, but only if his brothers earned it.

Unfortunately for them, Jacob (understandably) wanted no part of this plan. He had already lost one favorite son because his brothers couldn't keep an eye on him, and now Simeon was in an Egyptian jail. He wasn't about to go down that road with Benjamin.

Remember Reuben, the eldest brother whose half-measure helped lead to Joseph's plight? This time, Reuben stepped forward and took full responsibility for his brother's safety: "Kill my two sons if I do not bring him back to you. Put him in my hands, and I will bring him back to you" (Genesis 42:37).

What a heavy promise. Reuben prioritized Benjamin's safety over that of his own offspring. Here we begin to see a shift in the brothers' priorities.

Jacob resisted, but the famine continued and soon the family ran out of food again. The brothers were forced to return to Egypt to buy more, and they knew if they returned without Benjamin, they'd join Simeon in prison and all hope would be lost.

Even in the face of starvation, Jacob couldn't bear the thought of letting Benjamin out of his sight. Then Judah, another brother, made a promise: "I will be a pledge of his safety. From my hand you shall require him. If I do not bring him back to you and set him before you, then let me bear the blame forever" (Genesis 43:9).

Again, another brother was putting Benjamin's fate above his own. Interesting. Let's bookmark that.

Starvation forced his hand, and Jacob eventually had no choice but to relent. The brothers returned to Egypt with Benjamin in tow and bowed before Joseph (again fulfilling Joseph's dream). Joseph inquired about their father and, upon hearing he was well, looked upon Benjamin. Benjamin was the only other of Jacob's sons also to be born of Joseph's mother, Rachel, and the sight of him overwhelmed Joseph with emotion. He had to excuse himself to a private room, where he broke down and wept.

In Benjamin, Joseph saw himself from all those years ago: an innocent young boy, vulnerable and depending on his brothers to protect him. I imagine just seeing Benjamin took him back to that excruciatingly painful moment when he, in chains, gazed upon his brothers counting their money and rejoicing in the fact they'd never see him again.

Would they again betray their little brother as they had him?

Joseph had to find out.

He released Simeon and hosted his brothers with a grand dinner, "and they drank and were merry with him" (Genesis 43:34). Even as the group had a grand time, I can't help but imagine the pangs of sadness Joseph felt throughout the friendly meal; what if his relationship with his brothers had always been like this? This was the bond he had always wanted with them, and yet he only attained it when they had no idea who he was.

Despite the lively dinner conversation, Joseph had one last test up his sleeve: one that would determine if these broken relationships had any chance of being salvaged.

Joseph had been given a silver cup as a symbol of his authority; it was thought to have predictive, supernatural powers. Joseph didn't believe in such nonsense, but he was well aware that stealing such an item was a serious crime. As his brothers prepared to leave and the Egyptians filled their sacks with grain, he instructed that his precious silver cup should be placed in Benjamin's sack.

After the brothers left, Joseph sent his palace manager to catch up to them and accuse them of stealing the silver cup. The incredulous brothers strongly denied this accusation, saying that if the cup was found in one of their sacks, that brother should be put to death and the rest would become Egypt's slaves.

Unfortunately, the brothers didn't know about the plant. When the cup was found in Benjamin's sack, they tore their clothes in despair.

Here we see yet another sign of change. In biblical times, tearing one's clothing was a sign of deep sorrow and grief. Joseph's brothers were terrified of the fate that would now befall Benjamin, and they were beside themselves with anguish. They knew they couldn't return to Jacob after losing Benjamin, so they hightailed it back to Egypt to plead for his life.

Joseph continued the ruse, demanding to know why they would try to steal from him. Judah replied:

> What shall we say to my lord? What shall we speak? Or how can we clear ourselves? God has found out the guilt of your servants; behold, we are my lord's servants, both we and he also in whose hand the cup has been found. (Genesis 44:16)

If you haven't been keeping notes, these brothers appear to be very different men from the ones that betrayed Joseph. Joseph needed just a bit more evidence of their transformation, so he told them he would mercifully allow the rest to return to their father in peace, keeping only Benjamin as his slave.

Such a compromise would have been more than acceptable to his brothers in the past. They could have gone back to Jacob with another bloody robe, claiming innocence and moving on with life sans one pesky brother.

Not this time.

Judah threw himself at Joseph's mercy, launching into the whole story of Joseph's past and how, if the brothers returned without Benjamin, Joseph would essentially kill Jacob with grief.

> Now therefore, please let your servant remain instead of the boy as a servant to my lord, and let the boy go back with his brothers. For how can I go back to my father if the boy is not with me? I fear to see the evil that would find my father. (Genesis 44:33–34)

Those three sentences broke Joseph. More than twenty years

after Judah had brought up the idea of selling Joseph (Genesis 37:26), he now offered himself in place of Benjamin.

With that, Joseph ordered all his attendants out of the room so he was alone with his brothers, and then he hit them with the big reveal. The kid that his brothers left for dead all those years ago? Not only was he alive, but he had also become one of the most powerful people in the land.

As Joseph loudly wept, his stupefied brothers couldn't even utter a response.

Imagine the guilt, anguish, and fear that coursed through them as they realized this was indeed their long-lost brother. They had tried to get rid of him, and now he held their lives in his hands.

Revenge was his. He could deny them food. He could imprison them. He could even have them killed.

Joseph quickly dispelled any fear of retribution:

> And now do not be distressed or angry with yourselves because you sold me here, for God sent me before you to preserve life. For the famine has been in the land these two years, and there are yet five years in which there will be neither plowing nor harvest. And God sent me before you to preserve for you a remnant on earth, and to keep alive for you many survivors. So it was not you who sent me here, but God. He has made me a father to Pharaoh, and lord of all his house and ruler over all the land of Egypt. (Genesis 45:5–8)

With that, he sent his brothers back to Canaan to fetch Jacob and the rest of the family, who moved to Egypt and lived in the lap of luxury (Genesis 45:18).

All because Joseph prioritized his relationship with his brothers over any thoughts of personal revenge.

Think of all the years Joseph was enslaved and sat in prison, stewing over what his brothers had done to him. No one would have blamed him for building up a callous hatred in his heart, resulting in sweet, sweet revenge when his brothers were at his mercy.

Instead, Joseph opened his heart and allowed God to heal the wounds his brothers dealt him. Look again at the forgiveness he showed his brothers; three times, he said that God sent him to Egypt and used hardships to help him develop into the man he had become. Though his brothers meant harm, God had turned their intentions into a blessing for Joseph.

Joseph's brothers, especially Judah and Reuben, deserve credit too. They committed reprehensible acts, but they clearly changed and matured. They went from throwing Joseph under the bus to launching themselves beneath the tires to save Benjamin.

But Joseph wouldn't have known this had he not given them a second chance. His brothers didn't deserve it, but he showed them grace, and thus he was able to mend broken relationships.

Perhaps this chapter has brought to mind at least one once-fruitful relationship currently in tatters in your life. Maybe the other person harmed you in a way you couldn't possibly forgive. Perhaps you're at fault, and the thought of even facing that person again is too painful to bear.

And yet, God calls us to strive for unity, no matter how deep the wound:

> I appeal to you, brothers, by the name of our Lord Jesus Christ, that all of you agree, and that there be no divisions among you, but that you be united in the

> same mind and the same judgment. (1 Corinthians 1:10)
>
> By this all people will know that you are My disciples, if you have love for one another. (John 13:35)
>
> Do nothing from selfish ambition or conceit, but in humility count others more significant than yourselves. (Philippians 2:3)
>
> So then let us pursue what makes for peace and for mutual upbuilding. (Romans 14:19)
>
> Put on then, as God's chosen ones, holy and beloved, compassionate hearts, kindness, humility, meekness, and patience, bearing with one another and, if one has a complaint against another, forgiving each other; as the Lord has forgiven you, so you also must forgive. And above all these put on love, which binds everything together in perfect harmony. (Colossians 3:12–14)

The Bible goes on and on. Living in harmony is extremely important. Not only does it establish a familial atmosphere and loving spirit among Christian brothers and sisters, but it also inspires nonbelievers to learn more about the forgiving, loving family of Jesus.

This chapter should not suggest that it's easy to be like Joseph; on the contrary, it's incredibly difficult! Our selfish human nature creates friction, and like Shaq and Kobe, like Paul and Barnabas, we allow that tension to crush fruitful relationships.

If anyone had the right to break some fractured relationships, it was Jesus.

For more than two years, He had traveled with the apostles. He had taught them invaluable lessons and shown them miraculous signs. He had told them things He told no one else.

Most of all, Jesus was their ally. He had taken this lot of zealots, fishermen, and tax collectors that the rest of the world discarded, and He had befriended them. The things they had been through together should have created an inseparable bond.

And yet, the apostles' final hours with Jesus were a comedy of errors. After the Last Supper, Jesus and the disciples went to the Garden of Gethsemane. Jesus was in anguish over the coming events, so He sought solitude to pray to His Father. He instructed His apostles to wait while He prayed. This would seem like an opportune time for the apostles to pray too, or at least to discuss amongst themselves the things Jesus had told them at dinner and what they could do to help Him.

Nope. Three times, they fell asleep, leaving Jesus to face His toughest test on His own (Matthew 26:40–45).

Then a crowd of armed men arrived to arrest Jesus, sent by the leading priests and teachers of religious law. Other than Peter and John, the disciples hightailed it out of there faster than a dog when the vacuum cleaner turns on.

Then Peter, Jesus' rock (Matthew 16:18) and the one person He should have been able to count on, denied even knowing Jesus three times (Luke 22:54–62).

Despite everything Jesus had done for the apostles, they abandoned and betrayed Him when He needed them most.

And yet, look what happened the first time He met them as a

group following the resurrection. The apostles were huddled in a locked room, hiding out from the Jews.

> Jesus came and stood among them and said to them, "Peace be with you." When He had said this, He showed them His hands and His side. Then the disciples were glad when they saw the Lord. Jesus said to them again, "Peace be with you. As the Father has sent Me, even so I am sending you." And when He had said this, He breathed on them and said to them, "Receive the Holy Spirit. If you forgive the sins of any, they are forgiven them; if you withhold forgiveness from any, it is withheld." (John 20:19–23)

There's no anger. No hatred. No harboring of past wrongs. Only love.

Instead of showing the apostles the cold shoulder, Jesus sought them out. Rather than giving them the tongue-lashing they deserved, Jesus gave them His hard-earned peace, designated them as His messengers, and breathed the Holy Spirit into them.

Jesus should have questioned their loyalty and punished them. Instead, He rewarded them.

Now *that* is burying the hatchet!

And the amazing thing is that He'll do the same for you.

You may not have spent all those hours with Jesus physically as the apostles did, but you're just as much a child of God as they were. Just like them, you have sinned and given Him every reason to cut off His relationship with you.

But He hasn't. And He won't.

> Who shall separate us from the love of Christ? . . .
> For I am sure that neither death nor life, nor angels

> nor rulers, nor things present nor things to come, nor powers, nor height nor depth, nor anything else in all creation, will be able to separate us from the love of God in Christ Jesus our Lord. (Romans 8:35, 38–39)

It's a relationship impossible of being fractured. How can we respond to such overwhelming love? By doing our best to show it to one another.

> A new commandment I give to you, that you love one another: just as I have loved you, you also are to love one another. (John 13:34)

Jesus spoke those words to the apostles at the Last Supper. It was one of the last things He said to them before He was crucified. That's how important the message was.

As the Bible shows, God can make the most out of fractured relationships. He used Paul and Barnabas's split to multiply their reach. Only through his brothers' betrayal could Joseph find his way to Pharaoh's palace and save thousands of lives.

But it's better to forgive and salvage wounded friendships as Jesus did. Notice what happened to the apostles. When Jesus first met them after the crucifixion, they were terrified and cowering in fear. After He ascended into heaven, they received the Holy Spirit and became a powerful force ready to change the world.

It should be noted that Shaq and Kobe each went on to have very successful careers apart from each other. They both won NBA titles and earned their places in the Hall of Fame.

But their split will always be a popular topic among basketball historians. One can't help but look back on this once-great pair and think, "What if?"

CHAPTER 2

Distrust

Trust in the Lord with all your heart, and
do not lean on your own understanding. In all
your ways acknowledge Him,
and He will make straight your paths.
(Proverbs 3:5–6)

It was the fall of 2016, and everything was lining up perfectly for the Chicago Cubs. After winning 103 games in the regular season—eight more than any other team in baseball—they dismissed San Francisco and Los Angeles and advanced to the World Series.

But as much as I wanted to, I just couldn't believe they'd actually win it all.

I adopted the Cubs as my favorite Major League Baseball team because of my dad, who grew up watching the local broadcast of nearly every game. It was a nice father-son bond to share—except the Cubs were almost always terrible. Nicknamed the "Lovable Losers," the Cubs had last won the World Series in 1908. The following 108 years were a series of disappointments.

For the most part, the Cubs were just bad and finished near the bottom of the standings. Even in their best years, they offered just enough hope to cause searing emotional pain when they inevitably tripped just before the finish line.

Although the 2016 Cubs were supremely talented and came through time and time again in big spots, I couldn't quiet that voice in the back of my head that failure and pain were all that the future held.

And then it happened.

The Cubs lost three of the first four games in the World Series against the Cleveland Indians, but they rallied back. In the do-or-die seventh game, the Cubs scored twice in the tenth inning and pulled out an 8–7 victory.

Even after the final out, I watched the Cubs dogpile on the mound, thinking, "There's no way that just happened!"

Gideon would have made a really good Cubs fan.

Gideon

While this prophet acknowledged and respected God's power, Gideon needed frequent reassurance that God would come through for him. He never fully trusted until victory was secured.

We are introduced to Gideon in Judges 6, where we find God's people in a bad spot. The Israelites had become corrupt, so God handed them over to the cruel, slave-driving Midianites for seven years as punishment. These desert-dwelling enemies tormented the Israelites to the point of starvation, causing God's people to plead desperately to Him.

God's solution was Gideon, and He sent an angel to alert the hero of his mission. Gideon wasted no time in revealing his most irritating quality—distrust.

The angel appeared and said, "The Lord is with you, O mighty man of valor" (Judges 6:12). Gideon's response probably should have included at least one of these two elements: amazement that he was in the presence of an angel and stunned silence that an angel just gave him such an awesome compliment.

Instead, Gideon immediately questioned God.

> Please, my lord, if the Lord is with us, why then has all this happened to us? And where are all His wonderful deeds that our fathers recounted to us, saying, "Did not the Lord bring us up from Egypt?" But now the Lord has forsaken us and given us into the hand of Midian. (Judges 6:13)

Gideon should have understood that the Israelites were being punished for their wicked ways. They had earned their suffering. But Gideon questioned God's promises instead of realizing this encounter as a blessing. He should have responded with reverence, but instead he criticized the messenger of the very One who chose him.

To some extent, I can understand Gideon's hesitation. The Midianites were truly terrible; these marauders stole the Israelites' livestock and destroyed their crops, leaving them with nothing to eat. The enemy hordes were "like locusts in number—both they and their camels could not be counted—so that they laid waste the land as they came in" (Judges 6:5). Gideon was desperate and felt God had abandoned His people.

But again, Israel brought this upon itself. While we don't know exactly what the people did (it may have been due to idolatry, a common sin throughout the Book of Judges), it was clearly bad enough for God to exact some serious punishment. He didn't want to do this, but even as a parent must often resort to discipline to teach a child right from wrong, so God couldn't allow this disobedience to go unpunished. If God allowed this insolence to continue, He would have been doing His people a disservice. In order to achieve their potential (not to mention avoiding a fall into complete unbelief and damnation), the Israelites needed a wake-up call.

God responded, "Go in this might of yours and save Israel from the hand of Midian; do not I send you?" (Judges 6:14).

Gideon's head knew God was right, but his distrustful heart harbored more questions. Even though God's angel called him a "mighty man of valor," and God Himself acknowledged "this might of yours," Gideon conjured up excuses.

"Please, Lord," Gideon said, "how can I save Israel? Behold, my clan is the weakest in Manasseh, and I am the least in my father's house" (Judges 6:15).

Fear. Evasion. Disbelief. Gideon's immediate reaction was to try and get himself out of this position.

It's not an unfamiliar response. Many biblical heroes, such as Jonah and Moses, had similar initial reactions to God's assignments.

And the Midianites were a truly repulsive and dangerous people. Their numbers were great, and they swarmed their enemies as locusts onto crops, leaving only scant remains in their path. They were so fearsome that many Israelites chose to live in the wilderness, camping out in caves and mountains, to hide from them. Defeating this foe was no small task, and failure meant assured death. These people weren't the prisoner-taking kind.

But the Israelites wouldn't be alone. At this point, God had already delivered more than His fair share of surprising victories. In addition to getting Pharaoh to release them from Egypt and crushing the Egyptian army in the Red Sea, He had helped the Israelites score important victories over the Canaanites (Numbers 21:1–3) and the city of Jericho (Joshua 6). When Joshua, a God-fearing man, led the nation, Israel conquered the entire region and killed all the kings of those territories (Joshua 12:7–24).

God had even helped the Israelites previously defeat the Midianites (Numbers 31:1–12). With that list of military conquests, Gideon had more than enough evidence to have confidence in God's declaration.

God maintained His patience and replied, "But I will be with you, and you shall strike the Midianites as one man" (Judges 6:16).

End of discussion, right?

God assured Gideon victory. He didn't say, "I will greatly increase your chances of victory," or "You're better off with Me than without Me." He guaranteed a win. As God's hand-picked judge who was well aware of God's power and reputation, Gideon should have leapt at this opportunity.

Instead, he started what became a recurring theme: making God prove Himself. First, he asked God for a sign that the voice he was hearing was indeed God's (well, who else's would it be?). God passed with flying colors (Judges 6:17–21).

So Gideon gathered the Israelite army and prepared for battle. Then "the Spirit of the Lord clothed Gideon" (Judges 6:34), and warriors from surrounding tribes and nations sent soldiers to fight alongside Israel.

Our hero is finally confident, right?

Nope. He tested the Lord yet again, laying a fleece out at night and requesting that God soak it with dew but leave the surrounding ground dry. When God complied, Gideon requested the opposite the next night: wet ground, dry fleece. Again, God did as Gideon asked.

Asking for a sign is not a bad thing. In fact, it's very important to ask for wisdom from God. Great leaders such as Moses (Exodus 33:12–18) and David (Psalm 86:17) asked God for signs in times of trouble. When they were weary and beaten down by the world, God provided reminders of His power and grace.

However, we're also called to have faith in God's goodness, to trust Him rather than continually demand assurances of His power. God's patience can become tested when He's repeatedly asked to perform wonders. People constantly asked Jesus to prove Himself, and He got pretty tired of it:

> Then some of the scribes and Pharisees answered Him, saying, "Teacher, we wish to see a sign from You." But He answered them, "An evil and adulterous generation seeks for a sign, but no sign will be given to it except the sign of the prophet Jonah." (Matthew 12:38–39)

> The Pharisees came and began to argue with Him, seeking from Him a sign from heaven to test Him. And He sighed deeply in His spirit and said, "Why does this generation seek a sign?" (Mark 8:11–12)

> And the Pharisees and Sadducees came, and to test Him they asked Him to show them a sign from heaven. He answered them, "When it is evening, you say, 'It will be fair weather, for the sky is red.' And in the morning, 'It will be stormy today, for the sky is red and threatening.' You know how to interpret the

> appearance of the sky, but you cannot interpret the signs of the times. An evil and adulterous generation seeks for a sign, but no sign will be given to it except the sign of Jonah." (Matthew 16:1–4)

There's a difference between asking for confirmation that you should do something and failing to trust God. He had shown the Israelites His power. He had promised Gideon victory. And yet, Gideon demanded more, as if God's words weren't good enough. He even sensed he was getting on God's nerves, prefacing his final test by saying, "Please don't be angry with me, but let me make one more request" (see Judges 6:39).

Thomas is the biblical character that catches the most flak for doubting, but Gideon is right up there with him.

I almost want to laugh at Gideon's lack of faith, but are you and I so different? I cringe at the number of times I've checked my bank account and worried about paying bills, and yet I live a very comfortable life and have never even sniffed poverty.

For so long, I begged God for a sign that He truly did have a woman for me to marry. Though I doubted, He brought me Sarah, and she couldn't be more perfect.

Time and time again, God has shown me His goodness, yet I constantly seek more assurances. It's a convicting realization that I'm no better than Gideon—in fact, I may be worse. Gideon's people were at least oppressed by a hostile nation. I've lived most of my life in complete comfort.

Then I read Hebrews 13:5, and I'm especially convicted: "Keep your life free from love of money, and be content with what you have, for He has said, 'I will never leave you nor forsake you.'"

Go ahead and substitute any vice for the word *money*: power, position, status, and so on. God will always stick by our side. We don't need to ask for signs or promises, because we already have this declaration that He will remain with us in all circumstances.

It's also important to highlight God's patience. He gave Gideon sign after sign, even though Gideon shouldn't have needed any extra assurance. Yet the Bible doesn't record any annoyance or impatience from God. Like a parent patiently waiting for an anxious child at the bottom of a playground slide for the first time, He acknowledges our fear and does whatever necessary to assuage it.

When Gideon finally had enough signs from God, he set upon his mission to defeat the Midianites and free God's people. He camped his army of nearly thirty-two thousand near the spring of Harod, just a short distance from the Midianite army.

Now it was time for God to have some fun.

God told Gideon, "The people with you are too many for Me to give the Midianites into their hand, lest Israel boast over Me, saying, 'My own hand has saved me.' Now therefore proclaim in the ears of the people, saying, 'Whoever is fearful and trembling, let him return home and hurry away from Mount Gilead'" (Judges 7:2–3). With that, twenty-two thousand went home, cutting two-thirds of Gideon's army.

And God was just getting started. He instructed Gideon to take his men down to a stream and take a drink. The soldiers that cupped the water in their hands to drink could stay; those that got on their knees and lapped the water like a dog had to go. This test whittled the forces down to three hundred men, less than one percent of the original army.

The Midianite army had 135,000 soldiers, outnumbering Gideon's crew 450 to 1. Not even the greatest commander could overcome that disadvantage.

But that was just how God wanted it.

For all Gideon's tests, he now had to pass one himself. Gideon's men could not win this battle alone. Gideon would have to trust God to come through.

And he still wasn't confident.

Gideon snuck down into the Midianite camp with his servant Purah, where he overheard a conversation in which one soldier described a recent dream to another. His companion responded, "This is no other than the sword of Gideon the son of Joash, a man of Israel; God has given into his hand Midian and all the camp" (Judges 7:14).

With that, Gideon finally had all the assurances he needed.

That night, Gideon had his limited squad spread out and surround the Midianite camp. Once in position, Gideon gave the signal by blowing a ram's horn and breaking clay jars, in which were hidden torches. His hearty band followed suit, chanting, "A sword for the Lord and for Gideon!" (Judges 7:20).

The Midianite army, believing themselves to be surrounded by a massive force, rushed around in a panic. They were so frazzled and confused that in the dark of night, they began to fight one another, cutting down their own brothers. Gideon and his soldiers watched as the Midianites destroyed their own forces. Those who survived took off, with the galvanized Israelite army in hot pursuit.

The Israelites would have been routed in a traditional battle. Because of God's presence, they won without a soldier even having to remove his sword from its sheath.

As David put it so beautifully in Psalm 27:1, "The LORD is my light and my salvation; whom shall I fear? The LORD is the stronghold of my life; of whom shall I be afraid?"

Doubt is a part of everyday life. Even the most outwardly confident people constantly question themselves and those around them. God understands this. He's completely deserving of our complete trust, but He doesn't condemn our lack of faith.

Look at the first half of 1 Corinthians 13:4: "Love is patient and kind." Chances are you've heard that dozens of times at weddings, encouraging the couple to be forgiving to one another in times of strife.

But the verse also describes God's love. He cares for us so much that even when we stupidly doubt Him, He remains faithful to us.

Remember the feeling of riding a bike for the first time? It's a scary experience, filled with plenty of wobbling and likely a crash or two. But God is like the father with his hand on the young rider's back, helping him find his balance until he's comfortable riding without assistance.

God's love and compassion are beautifully displayed in the moments before Israel's attack. You see, it wasn't Gideon's idea to sneak down to the Midianite camp and hunt for intel. It was God's.

> Arise, go down against the camp, for I have given it into your hand. But if you are afraid to go down, go down to the camp with Purah your servant. And you shall hear what they say, and afterward your hands shall be strengthened to go down against the camp. (Judges 7:9–11)

Gideon hadn't asked for another sign, but God gave him one

anyway. He saw Gideon's nerves and gave his jumpy servant a confidence boost.

He didn't need to do that. But God loved Gideon, and He wanted His man to feel comfortable heading into battle. That's a knowing, caring God, right there.

While Gideon eventually was given the courage to trust God, we have every reason to believe God much more quickly. That brings us to a trio of men whose faith was more difficult to shake than it is to spell their names correctly.

Shadrach, Meshach, and Abednego

Things weren't looking great for these men at the beginning of the Book of Daniel. Babylon besieged and overtook Jerusalem, and its king, Nebuchadnezzar, instructed his chief of staff to sift through the prisoners, find the smartest, strongest young men, and bring them to his palace to be indoctrinated into Babylonian language and culture.

Of those chosen, one was Daniel, the book's author, of lions'-den fame. Three others were Hananiah, Mishael, and Azariah.

The Babylonians did all they could to rob these youngsters of their identities. They took them from their home, gave them new names (Shadrach, Meshach, and Abednego), and taught them the language and literature of Babylon. They even tried to drastically change their diets, though that effort didn't last long (Daniel 1:8–16).

The quartet excelled and progressed faster than any others in the training program, impressing Nebuchadnezzar. In fact, he found them ten times more capable than even his veteran magicians and enchanters (Daniel 1:20).

In disheartening circumstances, these four clung tight to the one thing Babylon couldn't take from them: their faith. God blessed them and helped them thrive; that is, until Nebuchadnezzar tried to steal their allegiance too.

Nebuchadnezzar thought himself a big deal—actually, a *really* big deal. So big, in fact, that he had a ninety-foot tall gold statue of himself erected. When his subjects heard the sound of musical instruments being played, they were ordered to bow to the ground and worship the statue. Those who didn't would be cast into a burning furnace.

The word *narcissist* doesn't even begin to describe this person.

This created a disturbing conundrum for the captured men of Judah. Exodus 20:3 ("You shall have no other gods before Me") strictly forbade them from glorifying this statue. But if they defied their new king, they'd become human barbecue.

It was an impossible choice: betray God, or die.

Given the dire straits, it would have been easy, even expected, for them to comply with Nebuchadnezzar's demands and justify their actions. If they bowed, God could surely sympathize with their situation. They could also bow while feigning reverence, only pretending to worship the idol. And if they refused to bow and were killed, pagans would fill their positions; wouldn't God want His people to hold authority?

No human would have faulted these men for taking the easy way out. After all, God is a merciful God (Hebrews 4:16; Psalm 86:5). It's not like they were abandoning Him forever.

Swallow your pride, bow, and live to fight another day.

We don't know what Daniel's status was at this moment. Having correctly interpreted the king's dreams (Daniel 2), he had been appointed as ruler over the province of Babylon and chief over all the wise men. He may have been away on business or deemed too valuable to incinerate, placing him in a different situation from his comrades. The Bible doesn't address his whereabouts in this story.

But Shadrach, Meshach, and Abednego were up a creek without a paddle. And when the music played, everyone bowed to the golden statue; everyone, that is, except three foreigners.

The king's astrologers and fortune tellers, jealous of these outsiders' rapid ascension up the ranks, were quick to tattle on the trio, who were summoned before Nebuchadnezzar. The king presented an ultimatum: one last chance to bow or become cinders. "And who is the god who will deliver you out of my hands?" he demanded (Daniel 3:15).

Shadrach, Meshach, and Abednego showed no hesitation in their response:

> O Nebuchadnezzar, we have no need to answer you in this matter. If this be so, our God whom we serve is able to deliver us from the burning fiery furnace, and He will deliver us out of your hand, O king. But if not, be it known to you, O king, that we will not serve your gods or worship the golden image that you have set up. (Daniel 3:16–18)

These three approached this impossible situation with a shared attitude: do your worst. You may take our lives, but you can't take our faith.

Imagine the pregame strategy these friends discussed as they considered the weight of their upcoming actions. I think Psalm 56:3–4 played heavily into their decision: "When I am afraid, I put my trust in You. In God, whose word I praise, in God I trust; I shall not be afraid. What can flesh do to me?"

If God is for us, who can be against us?

Compare this trust with what we witnessed from Gideon. Gideon needed sign on top of sign to prove that God would deliver him. Shadrach, Meshach, and Abednego asked for no such assurance. In fact, they even acknowledged the reality that God might not come to their aid.

But it didn't matter. Even if they went up in flames, the sacrifice was worth it. They would remain faithful whatever the outcome.

God doesn't always rescue those who are true to Him; this is why we have the term *martyr*. If God parachuted down to aid all His followers, we wouldn't need faith.

In Hebrews 11:1, faith is defined as "the assurance of things hoped for, the conviction of things not seen." If Shadrach, Meshach, and Abednego knew God would save them, they wouldn't be displaying faith. They'd simply be acting out of obedience, not love.

Religion isn't an insurance policy to deliver you from hard times. If it were, everyone would sign up. In fact, aligning yourself with God can bring additional hardships (John 16:33).

But our eternal reward far outweighs any earthly suffering:

> Blessed is the man who remains steadfast under trial, for when he has stood the test he will receive the crown of life, which God has promised to those who love Him. (James 1:12)

> Rejoice and be glad, for your reward is great in heaven, for so they persecuted the prophets who were before you. (Matthew 5:12)

> Do not fear what you are about to suffer. Behold, the devil is about to throw some of you into prison, that you may be tested, and for ten days you will have tribulation. Be faithful unto death, and I will give you the crown of life. (Revelation 2:10)

That's why Shadrach, Meshach, and Abednego, in the face of destruction, defied the one man who could save them out of reverence to the One who would redeem them.

Now let's talk about this furnace.

We're not talking about some rinky-dink home heater. This was an industrial-sized fire breather, likely used for making bricks and smelting metals. Even at its normal levels, the thought of survival in this oven was a laughing matter.

But Shadrach, Meshach, and Abednego's trust in God enraged Nebuchadnezzar past his breaking point. This egomaniac "was filled with fury, and the expression of his face was changed" (Daniel 3:19). He ordered the furnace to be made seven times hotter than normal. The heat was so overwhelming that the soldiers tasked with tossing Shadrach, Meshach, and Abednego into the flames were killed just because they got too close to the entrance.

Nebuchadnezzar gazed into the furnace to witness the destruction of the defiant men, except he saw three live men walking around. Or wait; were there four?

"But I see four men unbound, walking in the midst of the fire, and they are not hurt," he exclaimed to his advisers. "And the appearance of the fourth is like a son of the gods" (Daniel 3:25).

The king got as close as he could to the furnace and called for our heroes to come out of the flames. Shadrach, Meshach, and

Abednego emerged from the blaze completely unharmed. In fact, they didn't even smell of smoke!

The king said,

> "Blessed be the God of Shadrach, Meshach, and Abednego, who has sent His angel and delivered His servants, who trusted in Him, and set aside the king's command, and yielded up their bodies rather than serve and worship any god except their own God. Therefore I make a decree: Any people, nation, or language that speaks anything against the God of Shadrach, Meshach, and Abednego shall be torn limb from limb, and their houses laid in ruins, for there is no other god who is able to rescue in this way." Then the king promoted Shadrach, Meshach, and Abednego in the province of Babylon. (Daniel 3:28–30)

It's amazing how ego evaporates at the sight of God's righteousness. Not even the giant-headed Nebuchadnezzar could deny it any longer. He was dealing with someone greater than himself.

Shadrach, Meshach, and Abednego's trust paid off.

Despite no assurance that God would keep them from harm, Abednego, Shadrach, and Meshach (why does Abednego always have to be listed last? I'm switching things up for him) put their lives in His hands. And God not only delivered them, but He also (momentarily, at least) softened the heart of the king, thus influencing an entire nation. How many people came to trust God better because of their sacrifice?

So who was the fourth person in the fire?

We don't know exactly. We know that three men came into the furnace. We know that three men came out. What we're not sure of is who was the fourth man Nebuchadnezzar saw. He was obviously supernatural. Scholars debate whether he was an angel or a preincarnate appearance of Jesus Himself. Regardless, God sent a spiritual protector to place a shield around His three servants, keeping them from any harm in that impossible situation.

When Shadrach, Meshach, and Abednego responded in faith, God delivered.

So why is it so hard to trust Him sometimes?

One of my favorite all-time restaurants is a place in Omaha called Au Courant. Here, rather than ordering a specific dish, you're encouraged to order the chef's tasting menu. Over the course of an hour and a half or so, you're presented six courses, all from the creative mind of the chef and his talented team. You don't know what's coming until the plate arrives at your table and the server explains it; you put yourself in the hands of the chef.

I'll admit it was a bit intimidating the first time I tried it, but now I'll eat anything Au Courant places in front of me. I've eaten dishes with octopus, raw beef (if you haven't tried carpaccio, it's a must), crispy-skin trout, pickled beets, raw tuna—things I might not have been brave enough to order on my own. But I've grown to trust Au Courant's team of cooks and chefs so much, I'll wolf down whatever they recommend.

There's no thought in my head that one of the courses might stumble, or that a raw preparation might make me sick. I trust them implicitly to give me not only a great meal but also an eye-opening experience every time.

If I can trust a kitchen so boldly, why not God?

Think of the person that never lets you down. Maybe it's a parent who has been supportive through every season of your life.

Maybe it's a best friend to whom you can bare every portion of your soul. Or perhaps it's a teacher or professor who supported your dream. Maybe it's even the rock-solid closer of your favorite baseball team that never blows the save.

You trust these people because they always, *always*, come through. Until they don't, because they're human.

And that's always going to be the case. Because of sin, every human is fallen: "For all have sinned and fall short of the glory of God" (Romans 3:23).

You know whom you can trust? God.

Stop rolling your eyes; I know how cliché it is to say that. But sometimes clichés exist because they're true. The Bible makes it very clear that God is worthy of our trust:

> And we know that for those who love God all things work together for good, for those who are called according to His purpose. (Romans 8:28)

> Trust in the Lord forever, for the Lord God is an everlasting rock. (Isaiah 26:4)

> When I am afraid, I put my trust in You. (Psalm 56:3)

> Many are the sorrows of the wicked, but steadfast love surrounds the one who trusts in the Lord. (Psalm 32:10)

All things work together. Everlasting rock. Steadfast love.

When trials arise, these are the words you want describing your ally!

And yet, what happens when the fourth man isn't in the furnace? What happens when our enemies glance back into the fire and we're not walking around safely? What happens when the flames singe our skin?

What happens when God doesn't come through?

That's the question humankind has asked since the beginning of time. Scholars have pored over the Bible for the answer. Desperate, broken people have screamed it at God in frustration. Brokenhearted mourners whisper it as they walk by the casket.

Here's something I can promise you: whether you feel it or not, the fourth Man is always in the furnace with you. And that Man is Jesus.

In Mark 2, we find Jesus in a familiar position: swarmed by people. This was near the beginning of His ministry, but word had gotten out about this miracle worker. He had traveled throughout Galilee, preaching passionately and casting out demons. When Jesus arrived in Capernaum, a fishing village on the northern shore of the Sea of Galilee, everyone wanted a piece of Him. They descended upon Him like a swarm of hungry locusts, to the point where the place He was staying was so filled with people "that there was no more room, not even at the door" (Mark 2:2).

Quick side note: I absolutely love the patience Jesus displays here. He's coming off a trip where He was constantly mobbed by people begging Him to perform miracles. The poor man couldn't get a moment to Himself (Mark 1:35–39), to the point where the people flooded His place of residence. Imagine the Beatles' hotel room stuffed to the gills with adoring fans.

Jesus' response wasn't to seek solitude or to tell the people to give Him a minute. Rather, He taught them. He saw the value in this opportunity to change lives, and He prioritized that over His own desires. Pretty neat person, that Jesus.

Among the masses in Capernaum were four men with a paralytic friend. They had hoped to have Jesus heal their friend, but they quickly realized there was no chance they'd get to Him. Undeterred, they went to the roof of the house, peeled off a few tiles, and lowered their friend down on a bed.

Unfazed, Jesus accepted this unexpected visitor and told him, "Son, your sins are forgiven" (Mark 2:5). Then, "Rise, pick up your bed and go home" (Mark 2:11). And just like that, a man whose legs had not worked moments before, rose and walked out.

While Jesus was indeed compassionate, willing and able to heal anyone, the books of Matthew, Mark, and Luke all point out something fascinating: Jesus noticed the trust of the man's friends. In fact, the same verbiage is used in the three accounts: "And when Jesus saw their faith" (Matthew 9:2; Mark 2:5; see also Luke 5:20).

These men trusted Jesus to come through. They were willing to damage property and perform this desperate act because they had faith.

This story would have an awesome ending even if it only concluded with the healing, but the impact of this act didn't stop at the man's legs. "And [the man] rose and immediately picked up his bed and went out before them all, so that they were all amazed and glorified God, saying, 'We never saw anything like this!'" (Mark 2:12).

Others were blessed and chose to praise God because of this healing. They might not have believed in Jesus without it.

The paralytic had suffered for a long time. As a very active person and an avid runner, I cannot even begin to fathom what his sedentary life would have been like. His friends clearly were so disheartened by his suffering that they went to great lengths to get him to Jesus.

These five men appeared to be alone in the furnace. But there was a sixth.

The beauty of their story is that they realized they weren't alone! They believed not only in Jesus' ability to heal their friend, but also that He would be compassionate and loving enough to interrupt His teaching to do so. Faced with such incredible trust, Jesus was moved to respond.

As Gideon's story shows, God is patient with us. Even if we don't fully trust Him, He will still work on our behalf. That's how much He loves us.

But Shadrach, Meshach, Abednego, and these four friends prove that trust means a great deal to our Savior. Take note of Mark 9:23: "All things are possible for one who believes."

That doesn't mean that God will answer every prayer request with a yes. But we can be confident that He appreciates our trust:

> And we know that for those who love God all things work together for good, for those who are called according to His purpose. (Romans 8:28)

> You keep him in perfect peace whose mind is stayed on You, because he trusts in You. (Isaiah 26:3)

> Commit your way to the Lord; trust in Him, and He will act. (Psalm 37:5)

Rather than lay out another fleece at night, face the flames as Shadrach, Meshach, and Abednego did: "But if not . . ." (Daniel 3:18).

Don't waste your time and energy doubting Him or repeatedly asking for signs of His goodness. If God can deliver the Cubs a World Series, what can't He do?

CHAPTER 3

DOUBT

Rejoice always, pray without ceasing,
give thanks in all circumstances; for this
is the will of God in Christ Jesus for you.
(1 Thessalonians 5:16–18)

These words of Paul's first Letter to the Thessalonians are meant to serve as encouragement to a new church of young believers.

At times, they have had the opposite effect on me. Rather than uplift, those verses have momentarily made me want to put my fist through a wall and, even more destructively, question my faith.

I react this way because of my sister.

My sister is one of the strongest, most powerful people I know. A Christian schoolteacher, she's a daily inspiration to her students. She's taken countless friends to church, led Bible studies, and is a shining light to everyone around her. My sister is one of my best friends, someone I know I can confide in with even the most intimate topics.

She has a mild form of cerebral palsy, a condition that affects the way she walks. A series of surgeries in her youth improved the condition, but it's still a daily struggle for her. In addition, compensating for the condition has caused lasting pain and issues in other parts of her body, mainly her back. Though she resolutely charges forward and refuses to let her issues define her, she constantly battles an enemy she can't see and, more heartbreakingly, can't beat.

As a child and teen, I prayed for her to be healed every night. I tried everything, from quiet supplication to passionate pleading. My sister is such a good person, and it would take no effort from God to heal her. I would give one of my pinky fingers to let her experience a day in a perfectly healthy body. A simple thought from God would change her forever.

But nothing changed.

So I gave up. I'd had it. I didn't doubt God's ability to heal my sister. I knew He had the power.

But He just didn't seem to care. It felt like He just sat on some faraway throne, cold and unfeeling. Whatever healing my sister was to receive, it was going to come from some medical breakthrough or genius doctor, not God.

"Rejoice always"? Why?

"Pray without ceasing"? To what end?

"Give thanks in all circumstances"? I'd be thankful once God carried out His end of the bargain.

I bet you have felt something similar, probably several times in your life. Sometimes God feels so far away, more a concept than a being. The thought of an all-powerful God who loves us and is working for our good (Romans 8:28) sounds amazing.

So why does it always feel like we're waiting for Him to show up?

Where's God when we really need Him? When we get laid off?

When our significant other says she's leaving us? When we're suddenly presented with an unexpected medical bill we have no way of paying? When a dear loved one passes?

Where is God then?

Abraham

I imagine that's what Abraham was thinking as he awaited an heir. God made a promise to him, guaranteeing that he would be the father of a great nation. Yet as Abraham reached his mid-eighties, he and his wife remained childless.

While he wasn't perfect, Abraham clearly made an impression on his Lord. Back when Abraham was seventy-five, God had promised multiple times that his descendants would become a great nation (Genesis 12:2, 7; 15:18). In response, Abraham displayed great faith by leaving everything he knew and moving to an unknown destination, just because God told him to (Genesis 12:1–4).

But Sarah, Abraham's wife, was barren. Despite God's promises of this glorious line, Abraham and Sarah couldn't have a single son.

Go back to the last time you were passed over for something you were promised: that coveted promotion, the starting forward spot on the soccer team, that dinner with your child who never seems to have time for you anymore. That pain cuts deep, especially when it comes from someone you love and trust.

Abraham had shown God plenty of devotion in leaving his home to live as a stranger in a foreign land. Yet even when he asked God about that promise of children (Genesis 15:2), God just repeated the promise back again without further instructions.

Eventually, Abraham couldn't take it anymore. He let doubt seep into his mind and overtake the assurances God had promised him. Abraham and Sarah weren't getting any younger, and his line would die if he didn't have a son. And so, at Sarah's request, he slept with his wife's servant, Hagar, who became pregnant and gave birth to Ishmael. It wasn't the preferred situation, but now at least Abraham had an heir to carry on his line.

Unfortunately, this plan ran counter to God's. God had promised a son to Abraham. That's an unbreakable covenant from an unshakable God.

As Ishmael became a teenager and Abraham neared the century mark, God reaffirmed His covenant with him: "Walk before Me, and be blameless, that I may make My covenant between Me and you, and may multiply you greatly" (Genesis 17:1–2).

Abraham's response? He laughed in disbelief (Genesis 17:17). And later, so did Sarah (18:12).

Yeah, right, God. We've heard that one before. Still waiting.

Put yourself in God's shoes here. You've just told two people you dearly care for and have blessed greatly that you're going to come through. And they rolled their eyes and said, "Whatever."

I don't know about you, dear reader, but I think that response deserves a heavenly kick in the pants, not a blessing.

Despite their doubt, petulance, and defiance, God delivered. Sarah became pregnant soon after, and Abraham received his heir, Isaac, at the ripe age of one hundred years. Even when Abraham panicked and didn't hold up his end of the deal, God stuck to His oath. He showed no ill will toward Abraham. As promised, He crafted a historic line that included His own Son, Jesus, through His dearly loved servant.

God was very patient in this instance, but a lack of faith can get under His skin. We find a similar scenario to this in Luke 1, where the priest Zechariah and his wife, Elizabeth, struggled to get pregnant. Just like Abraham and Sarah, the couple reached old age and gave up on having children, until an angel appeared to Zechariah in the temple. The angel informed him that Elizabeth would become pregnant and have a son who would be named John. He would pave the way for Jesus' coming.

Zechariah, no doubt stunned by this sudden appearance and shocking news, could only utter, "How shall I know this? For I am an old man, and my wife is advanced in years" (Luke 1:18).

Wrong answer.

There are no limits to God's patience, but sometimes discipline is necessary (Job 5:17). His messenger had explicitly told Zechariah, a priest well aware of God's abilities and quite familiar with the story of Abraham and Sarah's miracle baby, that Elizabeth would become pregnant. And Zechariah's first response was, "Can you prove it?"

For his doubt, God took Zechariah's speech away until John was born.

I can imagine what you're thinking: those are great stories, and assuredly they prove God's ability to follow through on a promise. But very few people receive the angelic visit Zechariah did, much less a personal promise from their Creator. How can you be sure God is going to answer your prayers?

Here's some assurance: God hears and answers every single prayer (1 John 5:14).

However, that doesn't mean He'll always answer yes.

Sometimes, our plan isn't in accordance with God's. What seems reasonable, even downright obvious in our human minds, doesn't fit into His perfect design. There is no guarantee that your prayer, no matter how noble, will be answered in the way you want.

Mary and Martha

Take Martha and Mary. These sisters were close friends of Jesus who had shared powerful moments with Him. In John 11, their brother, Lazarus, had fallen deeply ill. Mary and Martha sent messengers to Jesus, pleading with Him to heal Lazarus.

If Jesus hurried and Lazarus could hold on long enough, perhaps He could reach Lazarus before His friend passed.

Unfortunately, He wasn't in much of a hurry.

> Now Jesus loved Martha and her sister and Lazarus. So, when He heard that Lazarus was ill, He stayed two days longer in the place where He was. (John 11:5–6)

Wait, what?

Jesus knew a dear friend was in grave danger. He had the power to heal him. Yet He decided to take His time rather than rush to his aid.

Jesus wasn't bound by the laws of humanity. If He wanted, He could have teleported immediately and been at Lazarus's bedside to heal his ailment. For that matter, He didn't even need to be there physically. With just a thought, Jesus could cure His friend from miles away.

But He didn't, and Lazarus died. Jesus let that happen.

Imagine the confusion Mary and Martha felt. Jesus was supposed to be not only their friend but also their advocate (1 John 2:1), their Good Shepherd who "lays down His life for the sheep" (John 10:11). But now it appeared that the Shepherd had fallen asleep and a wolf had picked off one of the flock.

When Jesus did show up, His arrival was met with high emotion. Mary fell at her Master's feet, but she couldn't contain her true feelings: "Lord, if You had been here, my brother would not have died" (John 11:32). The townspeople, too, were perplexed. "Could not He who opened the eyes of the blind man also have kept this man from dying?" (John 11:37). Doubt infected the crowd with a sense of finality: Lazarus was dead, and Jesus had let it happen.

But while the people were consumed by the present, Jesus saw the complete picture. When He arrived at Lazarus's tomb, He requested that the stone covering the opening be removed. He then prayed and called out to Lazarus, and the once-dead man stumbled out of the crypt, alive and well.

The story concludes with a happy storybook ending. But if Jesus intended Lazarus to come out of the ordeal healthy, why put his sisters through agony and grief by letting him die, if He intended to raise him anyway?

The ultimate plan is brought to light in John 11:45: "Many of the Jews therefore, who had come with Mary and had seen what He did, believed in Him." There was a reason for Jesus' inaction. The situation turned out to be a win-win; not only did Lazarus get to live (with a great story to tell, mind you), but also, more souls were saved. While Mary and Martha were hurt by Jesus' tardiness, His plan turned out to be far better than what the sisters could have imagined.

Jesus had the power and the desire to save Lazarus all along. For the betterment of everyone involved, He had to deny the desperate prayer requests of His dear friends.

For reasons we can't always understand, sometimes God just says no.

That's a really hard truth to swallow, and I feel your pain in accepting it. In good times, it's easy to look at Luke 18:1 and be encouraged: "And [Jesus] told them a parable to the effect that they ought always to pray and not lose heart." In this parable, a widow's persistent pleas for justice swayed a powerful judge to help her.

The takeaway: when life is hard, persistent prayer is the key. The squeaky wheel gets the oil, right?

"And will not God give justice to His elect, who cry to Him day and night? Will He delay long over them?" (Luke 18:7).

But when times are dark, it's easy to read that story and think, "Sure, that's easy for Jesus to say. He's not the one feeling my pain."

Except He did.

In the moments leading up to His arrest and subsequent crucifixion, Jesus knew the pain that was coming. He could hear each upcoming insult, feel each blade of the whip enter His skin, experience the horror of nails being pounded into His flesh before it happened. Not only would His friends betray Him, but they would also deny they even knew Him, in His hour of greatest need.

Worst of all, Jesus would have to carry the full weight of our sins and be separated from His Father for the first time. He pleaded for another way—any other way (Luke 22:42).

But as much as it tore Him up inside, His Father said no. This is how it had to be. A veil of sin had existed between God and humanity since Adam and Eve bit into the fruit. For it to be torn down, Jesus had to sacrifice Himself. There was no other way.

It was part of the plan.

If God is willing to deny His own Son, you have to accept that He might say no to you. Not out of spite, but for your greater good, as well as the good of those who will be impacted by your life, faith, words, and deeds.

That is not the most comforting statement to read, and it's not going to automatically erase your doubt when moments of trial arise. When they do, I hope you're able to return to these verses:

> Trust in the Lord with all your heart, and do not lean on your own understanding. (Proverbs 3:5)

> Do not be anxious about anything, but in everything by prayer and supplication with thanksgiving let your requests be made known to God. And the peace of God, which surpasses all understanding, will guard your hearts and your minds in Christ Jesus. (Philippians 4:6–7)

> He is not afraid of bad news; his heart is firm, trusting in the Lord. (Psalm 112:7)

God's answer to your prayers isn't always going to line up perfectly with what you had in mind. Often, you're going to be confused and disappointed with the answer you receive. But your Master asks you to respond in two ways:

1. Keep praying.

> Ask, and it will be given to you; seek, and you will find; knock, and it will be opened to you. For everyone who asks receives, and the one who seeks finds, and to the one who knocks it will be opened. (Matthew 7:7–8)

2. Trust Him when the answer isn't what you wanted.

> Now faith is the assurance of things hoped for, the conviction of things not seen. (Hebrews 11:1)

I don't know why God has chosen not to heal my sister (yet). To me, it seems like a slam dunk: after a lifetime of pain, an inspiring woman is miraculously healed from a thought-to-be incurable condition. Can you imagine the press that story would receive or the number of lives it would touch?

Maybe I'm not praying for the right thing.

In Matthew 8, Jesus is approached by a leper, a man covered in hideous sores and boils. He was an outcast from society, barely eking his way through each day with little hope for a better tomorrow. If anyone needed a miracle, it was him.

Yet look at what he said to Jesus: "Lord, if You will, You can make me clean" (8:2).

Not "Lord, please heal me."

Not "Lord, prove Your power and heal me!"

If you look closely, the leper doesn't even ask to be healed. He asks that Jesus' will be done. In that one sentence, he displayed a faith greater than anyone in the crowd at Lazarus's tomb: he admitted that the best path—Jesus' will—might not line up with his plans. He wanted so badly to be healed, but only if that's what Jesus wanted too.

Look how Jesus responded:

> And Jesus stretched out His hand and touched him, saying, "I will; be clean." And immediately his leprosy was cleansed. (Matthew 8:3)

Let's get real about leprosy: it isn't pretty. It often caused skin lesions, loss of hair, and facial disfigurement. The appearance of a leper was so appalling that in biblical times, the disease was considered to be a curse from God. Though it is much rarer now, in biblical times, leprosy was highly contagious. In Luke 17:12–13, we see a group of lepers who desired Jesus' healing but "stood at a distance." Even Old Testament laws decreed that lepers were unclean and should dwell outside the camp (Leviticus 13:45–46).

Needless to say, approaching a leper in biblical times was a major no-no. Best to keep your distance from the unclean, lest you bring their disfiguration upon yourself.

Yet we see no hesitation from Jesus. Picture this moment: the crowds spot the easily-identifiable leper and scatter, leaving the diseased all alone. In his shame, he desperately called out to Jesus in faith.

Jesus strode forth and did something no other person in the gathering would have done: He touched the leper. Jesus was moved by the man's belief and had no fear of showing His love for this person everyone else deemed unclean.

The leper's faith was rewarded with a personal blessing. Jesus loved him, looked past his rough physical appearance, and saw a believing heart.

The man asked for God's will, not his own, to be done. And he received a life-changing blessing for that faith.

Hard as it is for my human mind to accept, I recognize that my sister's resilience and iron will have been a blessing to many people. I live my life differently because of the example she sets, and I know I'm not alone in that.

I'm also strengthened by the assurance that my sister will be healed. Whether it comes in this life or when Jesus raises her to new life on the Last Day, she will be made whole. Though there seems a chasm of time between now and then, our time on earth is laughably short when compared to the eternity we get in heaven. Someday, God's answer to my prayer will be yes.

I'm going to take Paul's words to the Thessalonians to heart. Regardless of the outcome, I will be joyful. I won't stop praying. And I will give thanks for what God has given, while asking that His will, not mine, be done.

CHAPTER 4

FEAR

Fear not, for I am with you; be not dismayed,
for I am your God; I will strengthen you,
I will help you, I will uphold you with My righteous right hand.
(Isaiah 41:10)

I'm not usually one to brag, but I was pretty cool on the night I proposed to Sarah—up to a certain point.

It was a Friday, and I went to work as I would any other day. After work, I picked her up and took her to dinner at our special restaurant, where I wolfed down pizza and displayed none of the crippling nerves that often trip up proposals. I loved Sarah, and I knew she loved me. I felt nothing but confidence in our relationship and, more importantly, her. What did I have to fear?

But as dinner ended, that ring started to feel really heavy in my pocket, and my steely resolve began to crack. I started acting irrationally. It was the one-year anniversary of our first date, and our plan was to exchange gifts at a nearby lake. We agreed to freshen up in the bathroom before we left, but I instead went down to my car to have a minute alone to compose myself. When she came out of the bathroom, I was nowhere to be found.

My excuse for leaving her in the restaurant? I wanted to start the car's air-conditioning for her.

So smooth, right?

Then when we arrived at the lake, Sarah immediately spotted the photographer I had hired (fortunately, she didn't realize the photographer was for us).

My anxiety levels spiked.

The final touch came after we exited the car and entered the picnic area adjacent to the lake. I had met the photographer the night before and selected the perfect table to catch both the lake and the sunset in the background. But in the twenty-four hours since, a bird had died and now lay near the optimum table. Thinking with a clear mind, Sarah suggested sitting at a different table, as the area was nearly empty at that point.

But I, consumed with anxiety, kicked away the dead bird. "It's gone now," I concluded. "Let's just sit here."

Sarah looked at me as if I had just sprouted a second head.

Rational minds prevailed, and we sat on a bench free of rotting fowl. The proposal went off without a hitch from there, and though our photos had a parking lot in the background instead of a lakeside sunset, I wouldn't trade the story for the world.

It's hilarious to look back at this moment with hindsight. In those few moments, I was terrified. And I don't even know what I was scared of! I'm not trying to be cocky when I say I knew Sarah was going to say yes, but that doubt simply didn't exist. God had put this wonderful, beautiful woman into my life, and I into hers, for a reason—to love, strengthen, and uplift one another. I believed that with every fiber of my being, and she did too.

But fear isn't rational. It causes you momentarily to forget what you know to be unshakably true. Two plus two equals five. The sun rises in the west. Fact becomes fiction.

Jesus becomes just another man.

PETER

At least, He did in Peter's eyes for a few fateful moments. And Peter's fear could have cost him his life.

We pick up the story in Matthew 14. Jesus was putting the finishing touches on a sermon to more than five thousand people, an event that concluded with Him miraculously feeding the entire hungry gathering with five loaves of bread and two fish (Matthew 14:13–21).

This was not a sermon He had planned on giving. In fact, He came to this remote area specifically to be alone (Matthew 14:13). Unfortunately, His fame attracted the enormous crowd, and though Jesus felt compassion for them and was delighted to teach them, He was also anxious to commune with God. After He had fed the masses, He "immediately" told the disciples to return to their boat and sail to the other side of the lake, where He'd meet up with them (Matthew 14:22). Then He dismissed the satisfied crowd and went up on a nearby mountain, finally finding the seclusion He so desperately sought.

You know that feeling that sometimes comes on you where you just need to be alone? You get worn down and tired by people, even those you love. Sometimes you just need a mental break, if only for a few minutes, to regain your equilibrium.

Jesus, while God, was human too, and He had those same thoughts. Except He had twelve living shadows and attracted massive crowds wherever He went. Jesus desired one-on-one time with

His Father, someone He was used to being with constantly. Because He had set aside His divine power and glory, Jesus just wanted to recharge His batteries with prayer. This was that moment of escape.

It wouldn't last long.

A violent wind sprung up on the lake in the middle of the night, causing enormous waves and making the journey much more difficult for the disciples. As they fought to keep their course, Jesus appeared to them, walking on the water. So eerie was the sight that the disciples thought He was a ghost.

"Take heart; it is I," Jesus told them. "Do not be afraid" (Matthew 14:27).

This is an interesting moment for the disciples. While Jesus' ministry was still fairly young, they had seen Him perform a host of miracles, including healing a man from leprosy (Matthew 8:1–4), restoring motion to the paralyzed (Matthew 8:5–13; 9:1–7), and giving sight to the blind (Matthew 9:27–31). Indeed, the disciples had just witnessed Jesus feed a massive crowd with far less food than one would find in a typical pantry. Maybe the disciples didn't fully understand His mission yet (Matthew 16:13–20), but they knew something was clearly different about this Man.

This was the disciples' moment to prove they believed Jesus was what He said He was: the Son of God. But in their fear, most chose to cling to the mast or cower in the bottom of the boat.

Peter was the exception.

Like the rest of the disciples, Peter came from humble origins. He was a simple fisherman, but it didn't take long for him to separate himself from his peers. While they tended to be meek and passive, Peter was a man of action. He was usually the first of the group to speak his mind or act. Consider:

- When Jesus called Peter and his brother Andrew to follow Him, they "immediately" left their nets and followed Him (Matthew 4:18–20).
- When Jesus foretold His death, Peter so strongly denied this prediction that Jesus rebuked him and referred to him as Satan (Matthew 16:21–23).
- When Jesus predicted the disciples would all abandon Him upon His arrest, Peter was the first one to declare his allegiance (Matthew 26:31–33).
- When the Roman soldiers came to arrest Jesus, Peter drew his sword and cut off the ear of the high priest's servant (John 18:10).

Peter was often impulsive and immature, but he was also passionate. So when he saw Jesus on the water, His presence drove the fear from Peter's heart.

"Lord, if it is You, command me to come to You on the water," Peter said (Matthew 14:28).

This response could be interpreted as Peter testing Jesus, but I don't see it that way. Peter may not have fully understood Jesus yet, but he trusted Him. And now his Master was walking on the water, something no person had ever done.

Peter wanted to experience it. Who wouldn't?

"Come," Jesus said (verse 29).

With that, Peter arrived at a pivotal crossroads moment. Because he had been bold and trusted God, he had been given the chance to do something incredible, something Jesus had not invited the other eleven disciples to do. But it was risky; if Peter exited the boat and Jesus didn't hold up His end of the bargain, Peter was toast. Given the conditions, he'd drown in seconds.

Peter trusted Jesus, so he left the safety of the boat and began to walk toward his Lord.

Stop reading for a moment and try to imagine what this felt like: the surge that would go up your spine as you, not fully aware of what was happening, defied all laws of physics and walked on liquid. It had to have been the most exhilarating feeling!

But then Peter felt the ferocious wind. He noticed the vicious waves and registered the danger he had put himself in.

Fear hit him harder than a Muhammad Ali uppercut to the chin.

With his eyes off Jesus, Peter dropped into the waves, desperately crying out for Jesus to save him. Jesus grabbed His friend's arm and pulled him to safety, and the winds ceased as they climbed back into the boat.

Then Jesus, unable to hide His disappointment, turned to Peter: "O you of little faith, why did you doubt?" (verse 31).

Notice that the variables didn't change from when Peter stepped out of the boat to when he started to sink. The wind didn't get stronger. The waves didn't get higher. Jesus didn't move farther away.

Nothing changed except Peter's mindset.

In one moment, he was emboldened by Jesus' power. He had gotten a taste, but he knew there was more, and he wanted it all. Jesus awarded that faith with an incredible blessing not granted to any person before or since.

But then Peter took his eyes off what mattered. Instead of focusing on the One who had control of his life, he chose to focus on outside circumstances. His fear outweighed his trust, and that's why he failed.

You have probably felt something similar in your life. I'd bet you've seen God make powerful moves for you that should remove any doubt of His divinity and care for you. But in the midst of the storm, it's so easy to look away from Him and focus on the things that could sink us.

Finances. Unemployment. Anxiety. Loneliness. Pain.

In the moment, the pain from these triggers makes God feel so small. How can you trust God's goodness when you just got fired? Or got into a car accident and owe thousands of dollars you don't have? Or lost a loved one who died far before their time?

The waves seem so devastating, and Jesus so far away.

Ultimately, however, the long-term outlook doesn't change. Peter's steps as he made his way toward Jesus were not uniform. Some waves were stronger and hit his legs harder. Gusts of wind arose and threatened to knock him off-balance. Momentary obstacles made Peter's journey to Jesus more difficult, just as there will be potholes and flat tires on the road to heaven. It's inevitable; in fact, Jesus promises it in John 16:33:

> I have said these things to you, that in Me you may have peace. In the world you will have tribulation. But take heart; I have overcome the world.

Jesus knew trials would come. We must remain vigilant and, unlike Peter, resist the temptation to look down. Keep your eyes on the One who knows your glorious future.

Of course, that's much easier said than done. Even the most steadfast among us are going to feel the wind and the waves and question what's going on. What do we do when we begin to sink?

It's critical that we recognize Peter's response to his perilous situation: "Lord, save me" (Matthew 14:30). In desperation, Peter returned to the only One who could help him. He didn't possess the strength to stay above the water. The other disciples weren't about to dive into the waves and pull him out.

There was only One who separated him from life and death now: Jesus.

> Jesus immediately reached out His hand and took hold of him. (Matthew 14:31)

No hesitation. Peter needed saving, and Jesus immediately came to his rescue. He didn't care that Peter had failed, that he had spoiled this incredible moment. His friend needed rescuing.

I love that so much. Jesus was obviously disappointed in Peter. He had come so close to experiencing something truly special. If only Peter had stuck with it!

But even when Peter looked away, Jesus shot toward him, arm extended. He could have let Peter squirm for a second, maybe even let him experience the panic of sinking below the waves before saving him. That would have taught Peter the true difference between trusting Jesus and doubting.

But Jesus' love wouldn't let Him do it. His passion for Peter spurred action.

One might believe this was a life-altering experience for Peter. Given the way Jesus saved his sorry, unfaithful skin, he should have learned that fear isn't the answer. He should have become a sturdy rock, just as Jesus predicted he would be (Matthew 16:18).

Not so much.

On the night Jesus was arrested and brought into the high priest's house for trial, most of the disciples scattered in fear. But

Peter, true to his character, took a different path. He followed Jesus and the soldiers at a distance, anxious to see what happened to his Master. As Jesus was questioned inside, Peter joined the crowd around a campfire in the courtyard below to stay warm.

It didn't take long for the others to notice the outsider. Three times, Peter was asked if he was a follower of Jesus.

Three times, Peter denied not only being Jesus' follower, but even knowing Him (Luke 22:54–62). The betrayal is painful to read; it's the written version of fingernails slowly making their way down a chalkboard.

Being associated with Jesus was dangerous. At that very moment, Jesus was confirming that He was the Son of God, which was a blasphemous act to the Jews. In less than twenty-four hours, He'd be hanging from a cross, suffocating as nails pinned His hands and feet to the tree.

Under normal circumstances, Jesus was not an ideal friend to have. He was viewed as a revolutionary whose presence threatened to incite riots. Anyone who aided Him would have been viewed as a threat and could be subject to serious punishment.

Peter saw the peril that the risk presented, and he bailed.

When he realized that he had done exactly what Jesus predicted he would do (Matthew 26:31–35), he went away and wept bitterly, not to be heard from again until after Jesus' death. While Jesus breathed His last, hanging on the cross for Peter's sins, His disciple was hiding away, shameful and alone.

After Peter had supposedly learned his lesson, he let fear sink him again.

Much as I want to bury Peter for his lack of faith, I'm embarrassed to look within. Am I any different? I'm blessed with steady finances, yet I face a moment of panic anytime a larger bill comes up. My job performance is strong, but I've been laid off before; at any indication that my output is slipping, I immediately assume the worst is coming.

God has shown me His power and His goodness. So why can't I trust it?

Fear.

To be perfectly clear, fear is often a healthy response. If you were on a hike and saw a grizzly bear but felt no fear, you might end up as a midday snack. If you didn't fear, you'd cross the street without looking. You'd have no reason to wash your hands.

Fear is healthy. God designed it for a reason. It often helps keep us alive.

But it's only useful in applicable situations. For instance, if on that same hike you felt fear of a rabbit, that would be ridiculous. It would be foolish if you chose not to cross any streets, even if there was no traffic, out of fear that a car might materialize and flatten you.

Or, in a more realistic scenario, think about disease. Every time you interact with another human, touch a foreign surface, even breathe the air, you risk coming in contact with bacteria your body isn't equipped to fight. These can make you sick or even kill you. Fearing disease is perfectly rational and healthy.

But that doesn't mean you're never going to leave the house again, right? Doing so would ward off exposure to any unknowns, but you wouldn't be living! You wouldn't be fulfilling your purpose.

We can have worthwhile fears and still lead productive lives for God because we have confidence that He will protect us. Consider:

> Be strong and courageous. Do not fear or be in
> dread of them, for it is the Lord your God who

> goes with you. He will not leave you or forsake you. (Deuteronomy 31:6)

He goes with us. He won't leave us. He won't abandon us.

Want proof? Let's return to Peter.

After Jesus' death, the frightened disciples huddled and tried to regroup behind locked doors. Twice, Jesus appeared to them, assured them of His promise, and vanished again. These were encouraging yet brief visits that gave the disciples hope.

But I think He was saving His grand entrance for Peter.

Can you imagine the shiver that went down Peter's spine when he saw Jesus, even for just a few moments? Not only was he seeing a dead man, but also, the last time Peter had been in Jesus' vicinity, he had stabbed Him (metaphorically) in the back.

Befuddled, Peter did what brought him peace: he went fishing.

In John 21:1–19, Peter and several other disciples took their boat out on the Sea of Galilee but were having no luck. Suddenly, a voice called out from the beach, instructing them to cast their nets on the other side of the boat. It must have been an odd suggestion from a complete stranger, but the disciples complied.

Suddenly, their nets were so full, they couldn't get them into the boat.

At this point, John recognized the helpful stranger: "It is the Lord!" (John 21:7). Peter was so excited to see Jesus that he leapt out of the boat and swam to shore. Jesus had built a fire, and He cooked them breakfast with the fish they had caught.

After all, what better way to mend old wounds than through food?

But it wasn't going to be quite that easy. Peter surely still felt guilty about denying Jesus, a topic they had not yet discussed. This guilt could hamper Peter's effectiveness by making him feel unqualified to be the apostle God wanted him to be. After all, he had betrayed his best friend.

Rather than letting the issue hang in the air, heavy and unresolved, Jesus addressed the situation. It might be the only way to allay Peter of his guilt and empower him to reach his potential.

As the disciples polished off breakfast, Jesus singled out Peter: "Simon, son of John, do you love Me more than these?" Peter, desperate to prove his allegiance, blurted, "Yes, Lord; You know that I love You" (John 21:15).

But Jesus had heard this before. In Matthew 26, Jesus predicted that the disciples would all abandon Him. Peter piped up in denial: "Though they all fall away because of You, I will never fall away" (Matthew 26:33).

We saw how that worked out.

So Jesus pressed Peter. Twice more, He prodded: "Simon, son of John, do you love Me?" (John 21:16–17). I think He wanted to touch that nerve, to force Peter to revisit his most shameful moment. He needed Peter to understand that while he was forgiven, Peter needed to step up. His prior behavior wasn't acceptable.

Frustrated and ashamed, a grieved Peter exhaled, "Lord, You know everything; You know that I love You" (verse 17).

"Feed my sheep," Jesus replied (verse 17).

Three times, Jesus questioned Peter's loyalty, and the disciple verbally confirmed his dedication. Three times, Jesus responded by saying, "Feed My lambs" (verse 15); "Tend My sheep" (verse 16); "Feed My sheep" (verse 17).

Three times, Peter denied knowing Jesus, swearing and even calling down curses on himself. So three times, Jesus asked

Peter, "Do you love Me?" Jesus brought Peter back to that painful moment, the source of his greatest guilt, and restored him for the ministry he was to fulfill.

And for the rest of his life, that's what Peter did.

If only we could say the same for Pilate.

Pilate

Pilate allowed fear to be his driving force, and his lack of spine resulted in Jesus' death.

During Jesus' time, the Jews were under Roman rule. The Jewish leaders could arrest Jesus, put Him on trial in front of the high council, and beat and imprison Him. But they couldn't enact capital punishment without Roman approval. Pontius Pilate, the Roman official in charge of that administrative district, needed to sign off on any execution, including that of Jesus.

This was key. The leading priests and Jewish Council constantly butted heads against Jesus. They questioned Him (Luke 20:1–8; Mark 12:13–17) and accused Him of working on the Sabbath (John 5:1–16; Mark 2:23–24). And Jesus called them on their hypocrisy (Luke 11:37–54; Mark 12:38–40) and forcefully removed the merchants and money exchangers the religious leaders had allowed to conduct business in the temple (John 2:13–16; Matthew 21:12–13).

Oil and water, these two. And neither side was going to back down.

This brings us to Pilate.

After Jesus was arrested, the Jewish religious leaders quickly put in motion their treacherous plan to get rid of Him once and for all. All they had to do was rally a little public support. Once Jesus called Himself the Son of God (Mark 14:61–62), the religious leaders accused Jesus of blasphemy and had the people out for blood.

There was just one problem: Pilate had no quarrel with Jesus. When the Jews brought Jesus to be tried by Pilate, he couldn't find any fault with Him. In fact, the more time Pilate spent with Jesus, the more convinced he became that Jesus had done nothing wrong. Pilate's wife even had a terrible nightmare warning that Jesus was innocent (Matthew 27:19).

> You brought me this man as one who was misleading the people. And after examining Him before you, behold, I did not find this man guilty of any of your charges against Him. (Luke 23:14)

This obviously didn't sit well with the religious leaders, so they kept accusing Jesus. Seeing he was getting nowhere with these people, Pilate turned to his backup plan.

In those days, the governor had the power to release one prisoner of the crowd's choosing each year (Matthew 27:15). Among those imprisoned was Barabbas, an insurrectionist and zealot who had committed murder and tried to destabilize relations with Rome. His actions threatened the lives and political futures of the priests.

Knowing Jesus was innocent, Pilate tried to put before the Jewish leaders a less palatable choice: he would release either Jesus or Barabbas. He never guessed that they would consider Jesus, a peaceful miracle worker, as a more dangerous threat than the murderous Barabbas.

Guess which one the people chose.

Pilate went along with it out of fear.

Pilate knew Jesus was blameless. He admitted as such (Matthew

27:23). Yet as the crowd chanted for Barabbas to be released, Pilate sensed a riot coming on, so he called for a bowl of water. He washed his hands and declared, "I am innocent of this man's blood; see to it yourselves" (Matthew 27:24). With that, he released Barabbas and condemned Jesus to death. He thought he had put himself in the clear.

Nope. It doesn't work that way.

Jesus couldn't be crucified without a thumbs-up from Pilate. By declaring this innocent One guilty, Pilate was just as culpable as the leaders that put Jesus on the stand.

So why did Pilate do it?

Fear.

Pilate's primary job as governor of Judea was to keep the peace. Because Judea was so far from Rome and not viewed as a valuable asset, Pilate had limited military resources at his disposal. Historical documents indicate that Pilate was already on the hot seat due to prior uprisings in his region. If this situation turned into a riot, his job could have been on the line. The Jews knew this, and they even threatened to report Pilate to Caesar (John 19:12).

Fearing human judgment, Pilate abandoned his morals. He tried to turn the guilt on the mob by washing his hands of the outcome, but the decision was ultimately his. He was fully aware that Jesus was blameless, but he sent Him to His death anyway. As James 4:17 says, "Whoever knows the right thing to do and fails to do it, for him it is sin."

We all come to crossroad moments in our lives, in which we face the decision to do right or wrong. Often, the popular choice—what the crowd demands—isn't the right answer. It's hard to say no to people, especially those who directly affect our well-being.

But we're called to stand up and represent something higher. I'm not saying it's easy to choose Jesus over people all the time; in fact, it's often really, really hard, and Jesus promised it would be that way (John 16:33).

He also told us to take heart, for He has "overcome the world." In the face of any circumstance, I pray that you, dear reader, remember that and choose to honor God, not humankind.

There is no "washing your hands" of a decision. You ultimately must own each choice you make. Rather than bend to the will of people, carefully consider your big decisions and the lasting impact they will have.

Peter feared the judgment of other humans. Pilate feared a loss of power.

Neither of those compare to Jesus' sacrifice: loss of life and connection with His Father.

That's what Jesus faced in John 18. A crowd, led by His apostle Judas, approached to arrest Him just outside the Garden of Gethsemane. He knew the intense amount of pain, humiliation, and suffering the next day would bring; just moments beforehand, He had told the apostles that His soul was "very sorrowful, even to death" (Matthew 26:38). He had pleaded with God for the cup of suffering to be taken from Him (Luke 22:42). While He prayed alone, He agonized so deeply that "His sweat became like great drops of blood falling down to the ground" (Luke 22:44). For all that Jesus had experienced and endured, He was officially entering unknown territory.

Jesus was scared.

As two-faced Judas approached with a band of soldiers and officers, Jesus had the opportunity to consider other options. He could have run. He could have teleported Himself to safety. He could have called down an army of angels to tear His enemies apart.

The temptation had to be there.

But Jesus stood His ground.

Judas stepped forward and kissed Jesus on the cheek, a sign to the soldiers that this was the man to arrest. Rather than shove Judas away or give him a well-deserved fist in the kisser, Jesus looked at him and simply said, "Friend, do what you came to do" (Matthew 26:50).

When the soldiers surrounded Jesus, Peter drew his sword and slashed off the ear of the high priest's servant (John 18:10). Rather than take this distraction as an opportunity to run or join the violence, Jesus reprimanded Peter, picked up the man's ear off the ground, and reattached it to his head as if nothing had happened (Luke 22:51). Then He addressed the crowd:

> Have you come out as against a robber, with swords and clubs to capture Me? Day after day I was with you in the temple teaching, and you did not seize Me. But let the Scriptures be fulfilled. (Mark 14:48–49)

Staring down the barrel at His persecution, Jesus didn't blink. He didn't flee or attack. Rather, He healed one of His accusers and told them to arrest Him.

We might expect the human side of Jesus to be panicking, His nerves frayed beyond recognition. Yet Jesus was resolute, completely calm and collected. He didn't try to get out of the mission; in fact, He went out of His way to make things easier for His accusers.

What changed between the sweating of blood and this moment?

Jesus prayed.

He kept coming back to God. Three different times, He prayed the same prayer:

> Abba, Father, all things are possible for You. Remove this cup from Me. Yet not what I will, but what You will. (Mark 14:36; see also Matthew 26:39–44)

If there was any other option to save humanity, Jesus wanted to explore it. But notice that God never changed the answer. He never relented and said, "You know, this is pretty intense, isn't it? I bet we can find another way."

So why did Jesus' attitude change? How did He move from fear to courage in such a short amount of time?

Look at 1 John 4:18: "There is no fear in love, but perfect love casts out fear."

I think Jesus' communion with God refocused Him. Rather than concentrate on the suffering and death that awaited Him, He focused on love: God's love for Him, and His love for us.

When God didn't relent, Jesus was reassured that this was the perfect plan. In order to save humanity, someone needed to step in and take our place (1 John 2:2). He loved us so much that nothing was going to keep Him from His mission.

He replaced His fear with love and faith.

Ultimately, Peter did the same thing.

In the Book of Acts, we see Peter as a force to be reckoned with. Upon receiving the Holy Spirit, he delivered an impassioned speech to a massive crowd, turning three thousand nonbelievers to Christ (Acts 2:14–41). He boldly preached in the temple, at which point he was arrested and taken before Annas the high priest and his rulers and elders (Acts 4).

At this point, fearful Peter would have surrendered. He would have looked down and seen the waves. He would have sensed danger and denied Jesus.

But fearful Peter was gone. A bolder, more mature version ripped into the council of rulers and teachers of religious law, to the point where they were "astonished" at Peter's boldness (Acts 4:13). He so befuddled these scholars that they let him and John go out of fear that the people, upon hearing Peter's wisdom, would start a riot.

This was just the beginning. Peter had been emboldened, and he would never be the same.

Peter showed potential in the early parts of his life. Like I was in my proposal, he was perfectly confident when the going was easy, and he was more than willing to throw his support behind Jesus.

When the circumstances got tough, however, Peter tended to wilt. He depended on his own strength, courage, and cunning. It was only after he failed and Christ restored him that Peter understood the strength had to come from Christ and not himself. After Jesus' death and resurrection, and the outpouring of the Holy Spirit at Pentecost, Jesus empowered Peter to serve God faithfully in very trying circumstances.

Look at how God approached Peter. He acknowledged his failures. He called him out. But He still loved him, and He kept working on him. And in time, Peter became a faith-filled powerhouse.

I don't think there's a better way to sum up this chapter than with a note from Peter's own pen:

> And after you have suffered a little while, the God of all grace, who has called you to His eternal glory in Christ, will Himself restore, confirm, strengthen, and establish you. (1 Peter 5:10)

CHAPTER 5

Impatience

Whoever is slow to anger has great understanding,
but he who has a hasty temper exalts folly.
(Proverbs 14:29)

I will never forget the Christmas season of 2016. That was when I met Eve.

Eve was a Chiweenie puppy, a chihuahua-dachshund mix I got as a surprise Christmas gift in my late twenties from my then girlfriend. Eve constantly alternated between being precious and tender and deliberately insubordinate. She was a whirlwind of activity, always sprinting, barking, and urinating, sometimes all three at once. Picture the *Looney Tunes* Tasmanian Devil after chugging six Red Bulls.

In all honesty, Eve probably wasn't any more disobedient than a typical puppy. All young dogs require lots of training and patience. Unfortunately, I was suddenly a first-time dog owner working a full-time job, which meant a hyperactive canine version of Sonic the Hedgehog was cooped up in my apartment for nearly eight hours every day. As soon as she was released from her kennel, she ripped up towels, barked at her own tail (yes, that happened), and relieved herself everywhere.

Patience has never been a strong suit of mine, and this little stinker tested every last nerve I had. I would arrive home from a long day of work, hungry and mentally burnt out, only to find a turbocharged puppy in need of food, a walk, and some play time. And I couldn't even think about any alone time—the second Eve didn't receive attention, she began barking or biting my toes. If I dared try to discipline her—not in a physical way, but with training—she darted under the bed where I couldn't reach her.

Eve was an interesting challenge.

She tested my patience daily. Though I felt love and responsibility for her, there were days when I just couldn't deal with her. She seemed to save her most obnoxious moments for my most vulnerable, and though I never hit or abused her in any way, I'm not always proud of the language I muttered under my breath as I cleaned up another accident or chased her through the hallways of my apartment complex.

Through all this, my girlfriend and I tried to carry on a long-distance relationship, but the separation strained us. About a month after I received Eve, we broke up. She took Eve back with her to Wyoming, and I never saw the little pup again. The hurt from the breakup obviously stung, but there was also a touch of relief—while there were aspects of Eve's presence I would miss, she was no longer my responsibility.

Thank goodness!

Moses

I imagine that's how Moses often felt with the Israelites. Like I was with Eve, he had been surprised when a new responsibility was unexpectedly placed on his shoulders. But rather than one disobedient puppy, Moses had to shepherd over a million Israelites (Exodus 12:37–38) from enslavement in Egypt to the Promised Land.

Through a desert.

Over forty years.

I can't blame Moses for losing his cool. After all, this wasn't a mission he asked for.

But rather than be surprised by his girlfriend a few days before Christmas, Moses received his task from God Himself. Much as I cared for my lady at the time, Moses' assignment holds a bit more weight.

Moses' backstory is extraordinary, and I highly encourage you to catch up on his background in Exodus 1–14 (there's murder, a talking bush, an angel of death, and a sea splitting in half; trust me, you don't want to miss it). But we're going to jump ahead to Exodus 15.

The Israelites were slaves of the Egyptian empire for more than four hundred years, suffering the brutal wrath of Pharaoh, until God appointed Moses to free them (Exodus 3:7–10). Through a series of miracles, God helped Moses not only to convince Pharaoh to let the Israelites go (12:31), but also to deliver them to safety when Pharaoh changed his mind (14:5–31). As the waves of the Red Sea calmly settled to their normal levels, 600,000 men—not counting women and children—turned to Moses with the same thought on their minds: "Now what?"

The Promised Land.

The assurance of this utopia, this "land flowing with milk and honey" (Exodus 3:8), had long been a part of the Israelite narrative. The promise was first given to Abraham (Genesis 15:18–21), then confirmed to his son Isaac (Genesis 26:3) and grandson Jacob (Genesis 28:13). The people knew of God's vow, but now they were stranded in the middle of the desert with a leader they had only met a few weeks prior.

And so, after four hundred years of bondage, worked to the bone with no hope for a future, one might assume the Israelites would be thrilled to be rid of the whips, chains, and bondage they left behind.

It took just three days of freedom for the Israelites to start complaining.

Three.

Days.

To be fair, those three days didn't include any fresh water. And when God's people finally found an oasis, the water was too bitter to drink. The average human can only survive a few days without water, and these people were trudging through a seemingly never-ending desert.

On the other hand, they had just witnessed their God turn a river to blood (Exodus 7:14–25), blot out the sun (10:21–23), and crush their enemies under the sea (14:27–28). After all that, did they really think He was just going to abandon them in the desert?

Now put yourself in Moses' shoes. He had been perfectly content as a shepherd in rural Midian, living comfortably with his wife and her family. Then, upon a call from God, he risked everything, openly challenging and even threatening the most powerful man in the land for these people's sake.

And now they wanted to complain.

Lucky for them, Moses was the patient type. He cried to the Lord for help, and God made the water drinkable. Problem solved.

Oh, but things were only just getting started.

About forty-five days into the journey, the people moaned about the lack of food. "Would that we had died by the hand of the LORD in the land of Egypt, when we sat by the meat pots and ate bread to the full, for you have brought us out into this wilderness to kill this whole assembly with hunger" (Exodus 16:3). So God sent quail and created manna, a bread that appeared each morning on the desert floor. Every family had exactly enough food to eat (Exodus 16:4–17).

Then they got thirsty and complained against Moses again, this time to the point that he felt his life was threatened. "Why did you bring us up out of Egypt, to kill us and our children and our livestock with thirst?" they demanded (Exodus 17:3).

So God used Moses' staff to split open a rock and miraculously deliver water (Exodus 17:1–6).

Time and time again, the Israelites conveniently forgot the horrific past they had escaped and whined about the present. Moses took the brunt of their unhappiness, though the peoples' afflictions were no fault of his own. Each time, he patiently presented the Israelites' plight before the Lord.

In fact, on more than one occasion, God got so fed up with His chosen people that He considered wiping them out (Numbers 11:1–2; 14:11–20). Had Moses not been there to plead on their behalf, the Israelites might have gotten a firsthand taste of God's just wrath (Romans 2:5; Psalm 7:11).

Moses was the picture of patience, the tolerant leader of squabbling children. How does he maintain such an air of calm when faced with waves of nonsensical griping?

Look more closely at Moses' response to each situation:

> And [Moses] cried to the LORD, and the LORD showed him a log, and he threw it into the water, and the water became sweet. (Exodus 15:25)

> Then the LORD said to Moses, "Behold, I am about to rain bread from heaven for you." (Exodus 16:4)

> So Moses cried to the LORD, "What shall I do with this people? They are almost ready to stone me." (Exodus 17:4)

Moses was only able to maintain his sanity because each time the Israelites pushed him to the brink, he came to the Lord. Rather than rely on his own strength, he convened with God. And each time, God came through for him.

But even the strongest of us reach a breaking point.

Fast-forward to Numbers 20. The Israelites have been wandering in the desert for forty years since the exodus from Egypt (though thirty-seven of those were their own doing, as outlined in Numbers 13–14). Moses had stood strong with these malcontents for four faithful decades.

But all those years of complaining chipped away at Moses' resolve. Then Miriam, Moses' older sister, died. Along with Aaron, she had been at Moses' side for every step of this long journey. A faithful ally and valued family member was lost.

Moses was hurting, in desperate need of a day off, but the Israelite Complaint Committee would grant him no such luxury.

The Israelites made camp at Kadesh, just off the edge of the Promised Land. The arduous journey was nearly over, but the Israelites, true to form, lamented the lack of water:

> Would that we had perished when our brothers perished before the LORD! Why have you brought the assembly of the LORD into this wilderness, that we should die here, both we and our cattle? And why have you made us come up out of Egypt to bring us to this evil place? It is no place for grain or figs or vines or pomegranates, and there is no water to drink. (Numbers 20:3–5)

Look back through the past few pages and see how many times the Israelites chastised Moses for leading them out of Egypt—you know, risking everything to save their sorry skins. Without him, they would never have escaped the Egyptians' whips, much less navigated the desert to reach the Promised Land.

Again, Moses and Aaron faithfully fell face down before God. The Lord instructed Moses to speak to a rock, which would spew enough water for the entire community and livestock.

But Moses' patience was spent. He gathered the assembly in front of the rock and scolded them. "Hear now, you rebels: shall we bring water for you out of this rock?" (verse 10). With that, he angrily struck the rock with his staff twice. Fresh water erupted from stone, enough for all to be satisfied.

But in the midst of that miracle, Moses fell victim to the enemy he had held at bay for so many years: impatience. In his frustration, he took matters into his own hands. Self-control gave way to anger, causing him to claim responsibility for the miracle: "Shall *we* bring water for you out of this rock?" (emphasis added).

Moses took ownership of God's power. The Israelites finally broke him, and this momentary slip in patience shifted the spotlight onto him instead of on God.

Now, God isn't a prima donna who helps us solely for recognition or love. He's not that petty. But if a human uses God's power to steal glory or accolades for himself, it understandably rubs Him the wrong way.

Consider the following verses:

> Not to us, O Lord, not to us, but to Your name give glory, for the sake of Your steadfast love and Your faithfulness! (Psalm 115:1)

> Worthy are You, our Lord and God, to receive glory and honor and power, for You created all things, and by Your will they existed and were created. (Revelation 4:11)

In a moment of irritation, Moses forgot these truths, and it cost him dearly.

> And the Lord said to Moses and Aaron, "Because you did not believe in Me, to uphold Me as holy in the eyes of the people of Israel, therefore you shall not bring this assembly into the land that I have given them." (Numbers 20:12)

After all those years of enduring the nagging, slandering, and rebelling from the Israelites, that was it for Moses. He had led God's people on the long journey, but he wouldn't see the finish line. That one moment of weakness doomed him.

Moses' failure parallels something Jesus would tell a crowd on the Mount of Olives hundreds of years later. His message was grim, filled with warnings of the coming lies, struggles, and evil that would cause many believers to leave the faith (Matthew 24).

But He also spoke a word of hope: "But the one who endures to the end will be saved" (Matthew 24:13).

Moses couldn't quite endure to the end. He got so close, but he couldn't quite reach the destination for which he had worked so long and hard.

At first glance, this seems completely unfair. Moses had been God's rock. Other than initial hesitation about accepting the mission, Moses was a biblical superstar who carried out God's plan with almost no questions asked. He was as faithful as they come, even as his character and wisdom were attacked and chastised by Pharaoh (Exodus 10:10, 28), the Israelites (Exodus 16:3; Numbers 14:2), and even his own family (Numbers 12:1–3). He was, according to Numbers 12:3, "very meek, more than all people who were on the face of the earth." He gave God all the glory while enduring the barbs of both his friends and enemies.

So why, after a lifetime of successes and an iron-clad track record of patience, was Moses denied entrance to the Promised Land?

I think it comes down to one critical concept in Numbers 20:12: *trust*.

The Israelites' biggest problem was that they didn't trust God's power. Rather than have faith in God's love for them, they constantly doubted His plan and worried about their food, water, and military prowess. Their lack of faith caused them to wander the wilderness for an additional thirty-seven years (Numbers 13:25–14:38).

When Moses struck the rock with his staff, he displayed the same unfaithfulness that plagued his whiny followers. He didn't doubt that simply speaking to the rock would make it gush forth;

he had seen enough of God's power to acknowledge that. But his frustration caused him to doubt it would change the minds of the Israelites. Even if his words coaxed water from the rock, he'd just have to do this again and again and again, just as he had done so many times before. He was stuck in a desert *Groundhog Day*, a maddening loop of ungratefulness.

His whole life had been building to this moment. God had been developing Moses' patience all along. As God administered the ten plagues against Egypt, Moses had to wait patiently for Pharaoh's steely resolve to break (Exodus 7:14–33). As the Egyptians cornered the panicked Israelites at the Red Sea, Moses had to wait for God to part the waters and deliver them (Exodus 14). And as the freed Israelites complained about every grain of sand that found its way into their sandals, Moses had to hold firm, at the risk of losing his sanity.

Moses had been groomed for this final test! Pass it, and he got a ticket to the Promised Land.

Look at James 1:2–4:

> Count it all joy, my brothers, when you meet trials of various kinds, for you know that the testing of your faith produces steadfastness. And let steadfastness have its full effect, that you may be perfect and complete, lacking in nothing.

Moses faced many trials, more than most people could bear. Through them, God raised up a man capable of delivering His people from bondage. Moses' actions and leadership set the stage for David's lineage, which included Jesus.

But he failed.

This is all rather depressing, isn't it? The takeaway here seems to be that we can live a life devoted to God filled with great works, all of which can be undone by one mistake.

As we close out Moses' story, I want to make two points to dispel that thought.

First, our sins have been wiped out by Jesus' death and resurrection. He tore down the veil between us and God (Mark 15:38), and His Spirit sanctifies us (Hebrews 10:10). Because we have Jesus, we have life and access to God:

> Jesus said to him, "I am the way, and the truth, and the life. No one comes to the Father except through Me." (John 14:6)

Because of Jesus' sacrifice, the millions of mistakes you will make on earth won't separate you from the true promised land: heaven.

Second, we see how God really felt about Moses in their final interaction. You'd think God would be furious with Moses, beside Himself that His hand-picked leader succumbed to the temptation to lash out, enraged that this tiny human would claim God's power as his own.

But that's not what we see in Deuteronomy 34. As Moses neared the end of his life, God led him to the top of Mount Nebo, a peak that provided an aerial view of the entire Promised Land. "This is the land of which I swore to Abraham, to Isaac, and to Jacob, 'I will give it to your offspring,'" God said in Deuteronomy 34:4. "I have let you see it with your eyes, but you shall not go over there." And with that, Moses died at the ripe age of 120.

My first inclination is to think God is rubbing Moses' failure in his face. It's like showing Bill Buckner, the Major League Baseball All-Star whose famous error played a large part in the Boston Red

Sox losing the 1986 World Series, the championship trophy and saying, "Look what you could have had if you fielded that simple grounder. What a shame."

But God's next action showed he wasn't pouring salt in Moses' wound. After Moses passed, God buried him personally, an honor bestowed upon no other human. Despite His disappointment, God compassionately laid His friend to rest and welcomed him into heaven. Great as the Promised Land was from an earthly perspective, Moses was now truly in paradise.

God shared a relationship with Moses that He didn't have with any other human. Moses was the only person to speak with God face-to-face (Exodus 33:11; Numbers 12:8). These two had shared a century of adventures together. They relationship was forged through an escape from Egypt, a journey through the desert, and everything in between.

So when God showed Moses the Promised Land, He wasn't chastising him. God was lamenting: "Look at what we could have shared, My friend! I truly wish we could have experienced it together!" Though that was no longer the case, God still wanted Moses at least to see the land once before he passed.

God is just and doesn't play favorites. By His very nature, He must respond when the Law is disobeyed (Psalm 25:8–10). But He can also see our hearts, and ultimately, He is rooted in love.

God will hold us accountable. But at the end of it all, He'll just hold *us*.

That, for me, is the ultimate takeaway from Moses' story. His impatience caused him to commit a sin God deemed unfit for entering the Promised Land.

But Moses got something even better than a home in the land

of milk and honey. He got a personal relationship with God, a bond that was so strong that God personally laid him to rest.

I can picture the skeptic reading this chapter and thinking, "Well, great for Moses. But I'm never going to speak to a burning bush or lead a nation. God and Moses were best friends; what does Moses' story have to do with me?"

Let's take a look at Jesus.

We could point out plenty of instances in which Jesus showed patience. For example, He told His twelve closest companions multiple times that He was going to die (Matthew 16:21; 20:17–19; Mark 9:30–31), and yet they couldn't get the message through their thick skulls (Mark 9:32). Jesus was patience personified.

I want to look at a particular passage to point out His poise. In Luke 8, Jesus had just exorcised demons from a man. He and the apostles then sailed to the other side of the lake, where He was immediately mobbed by yet another crowd. As the swarm of humanity engulfed Jesus, a man named Jairus fell at His feet and begged Jesus to come to his home and heal his twelve-year-old daughter. Compassionate as ever, Jesus went with the man, wading through the dense crowd.

Among the masses was a woman who had suffered from constant bleeding for twelve years. Her life was a hopeless cycle of pain and impurity, but she recognized an opportunity to escape it. She fought her way through the crowd and managed to touch the edge of Jesus' robe. Immediately, her bleeding ceased and she was well.

Jesus felt the power go out of Him and stopped. "Who was it that touched Me?" (Luke 8:45). This query made no sense to the disciples. There was a massive crowd surrounding them; lots of people were touching Jesus. Why was He asking about one?

"Peter said, 'Master, the crowds surround You and are pressing in on You!' But Jesus said, 'Someone touched Me, for I perceive that power has gone out from Me'" (Luke 8:45–46).

Put yourself in this woman's shoes. She surely felt not only elation that she was healed, but also dread. In her eyes, she had taken power from Jesus. And He didn't appear too happy about it.

So she fell before Him, trembling with fear. She explained why she had touched Him and how she had been healed.

Now let's look at this encounter from Jesus' perspective. He is constantly mobbed by people everywhere He goes. He intentionally tried to find time to steal away from the crowds and be alone with God (John 6:15; Luke 5:15–16). Everyone was always demanding something from Him. The people wanted miracles and healing. The Pharisees wanted to question Him. The apostles wanted wisdom and knowledge. It had to be exhausting.

Now here was this woman, just another in a long line of people who didn't want Jesus, but wanted something *from* Him.

Or so it seemed.

In fact, this woman displayed incredible faith. One can only imagine how hard it would be to fight through this crowd to get in the remote vicinity of Jesus, much less with a physical affliction. To do so would require incredible faith—not a blind hope that Jesus would magically unleash a healing spell, but a genuine belief that He not only could, but would, remedy this incurable issue.

When the woman fell at Jesus' feet, she likely expected a scolding or punishment. She felt the need to justify her actions.

No such explanation was necessary.

Jesus said, "Daughter, your faith has made you well; go in peace" (Luke 8:48).

No damnation. No retribution. No chiding.

Instead, Jesus gave this stranger a blessing. And He called her *daughter.*

Just as Moses was constantly bombarded with demands from the Jewish people, Jesus was always surrounded by people who needed something from Him. Even as He performed this miracle, He was heading off to heal Jairus's daughter. As compassionate as Jesus was, I can only imagine He would have appreciated a break every once in a while. If anyone had the right to be impatient, it was Jesus.

But when He sought out the person who had used His power, He didn't do it in aggravation or anger. He wanted to meet this person of great faith and bless them.

This was just like God sitting with Moses, gazing out upon the Promised Land: "I love you, and while I know you're not perfect, I want to bless you."

Patience is a love language (1 Corinthians 13:4) that God calls us to keep constantly at the front of our minds. But just as Moses failed with the Israelites (and I did with Eve more than a few times), He knows we're fallen. We're going to give into impatience. We're going to fail.

Despite that, your name is on heaven's guest list, and you have a permanent spot if you want it.

God has displayed the ultimate patience with you. Why not share that same compassion with others?

CHAPTER 6

LUKEWARM LIVING

I know your works: you are neither cold nor hot.
Would that you were either cold or hot!
So, because you are lukewarm, and neither
hot nor cold, I will spit you out of My mouth.
(Revelation 3:15–16)

As an avid foodie, I've eaten thousands of meals in restaurants. The vast majority of those experiences have been tremendous. A few were, well, not so great.

But there is one that stands out from the rest of the pack—and not in a good way.

My dad and I were in Lincoln for a Nebraska basketball game, and I took him to an Irish pub at which I previously had nothing but great experiences. But as I took my first bite into my bacon cheeseburger, I knew something was wrong.

The patty was cold.

Not kind of cool.

Ice cold.

Ever optimistic, I hoped the dish could be salvaged. The restaurant was busy, and it was possible there had been some miscommunication in the kitchen. If the cooks threw the patty back on the grill for a few minutes, this beefy ice cube might be saved. I informed our waitress, who was very friendly and attentive, of the situation.

"No problem!" she beamed. "I'll throw that in the microwave for a few minutes and be right back!"

Wait, what?

I was so stunned that I couldn't even respond before she had whisked my burger away for a date in the zapper. Dad just started laughing. There was really no other response.

The burger returned as I expected: overcooked, tough, and borderline inedible. I had originally expected it would be served hot, and at least when it was cold I had hopes for a revival.

But this warmed mishmash of beef, bacon, and bun was completely unappealing.

That's how God feels about the lukewarm Christian. Those that run hot are consistently in the Word and communicate regularly with God. As a result, they're ready and available to serve God in every situation and win more souls for the kingdom. The cold unbelievers may not be ready to contribute to the cause, but they have potential if someone or something brings them to the Gospel of Christ—a church message, podcast, blog post, Bible study, and so on. The Holy Spirit uses His Word to fan the flames of our love for Christ.

The problem lies with the lukewarm—those Christians who profess to have a faith, but they don't really know Jesus Christ and what faith really is. They're often more preoccupied with pleasures, concerns, or worries of this life. They may go to church. They may be in a Bible study. These are wonderful practices that enrich both individual believers and the church community as a whole.

But if you ask their co-workers, friends, and family about their faith life, they wouldn't know how to answer.

An indifferent believer is repugnant to God. That may sound harsh, but His Word says He will spit out the lukewarm. Idle Christians are too comfortable in their current state to make a difference for the Kingdom.

The idea of lukewarm Christians makes me think of the zoo. Much as I enjoy the opportunity to view the majestic beauty of God's creatures and appreciate the conservation efforts of zoos, seeing animals in containment makes me a bit sad. I find it sobering to watch tigers pace back and forth behind the glass or polar bears lounge all day on faux boulders. These are amazing, perfectly engineered creatures designed to run, climb, explore, and live free. Instead, they're reduced to viewing fodder for a few moments until we move on to the next curiosity.

This is what the Holy Spirit is like in a lukewarm Christian. When unleashed, the Holy Spirit is a powerful ally (Acts 1:8; Romans 15:13) who teaches us, guides our steps, and empowers us for amazing lives of service to God and His world. But in the indifferent believer, He lies dormant, just dying to come forward and show us who Christ really is.

The Rich Young Man

Jesus encountered the ultimate lukewarm Christian late in His ministry. We know very little about this man; in fact, the Bible doesn't even disclose his name. All it takes, however, is a few verses to see that he was bursting at the seams with potential. But his half-hearted spirit squashed his ability to make a meaningful difference for the Kingdom.

As Jesus and His disciples made their fateful trip to Jerusalem, they were approached on the road by a young man. Luke's version refers to him as "a ruler" (Luke 18:18), and every account reveals that the man was rich. Though he was a man of influence and power, he approached Jesus with great humility and fell to his knees in front of Him. "Good Teacher, what must I do to inherit eternal life?" he asked (Mark 10:17).

Jesus loved the man deeply, but He knew the man was really asking, "What must I do to *earn* eternal life?" He had entirely missed Jesus' point: eternal life is a gift God gives freely through faith in Jesus Christ.

Jesus let the young man's thinking play out. He said, "You know the commandments: 'Do not murder, Do not commit adultery, Do not steal, Do not bear false witness, Do not defraud, Honor your father and mother'" (verse 19).

"Teacher," the man earnestly responded, "all these I have kept from my youth" (verse 20).

So far, this man appeared to be the opposite of lukewarm. First, he was a man of great influence who was willing to admit Jesus' divinity publicly, even bowing before Him. Such an action would have been heavily frowned upon by the religious leaders, most of whom would rather lick the bottom of their sandals than give Jesus a compliment, much less fall to their knees before Him. The man was well-versed in Scripture and was confident enough to claim he kept God's commandments. Jesus looked at him and loved him (verse 21). This guy had it all.

Or so it seemed.

Jesus told him, "You lack one thing: go, sell all that you have and give to the poor, and you will have treasure in heaven; and come, follow Me" (verse 21). It was a simple test of the First Commandment—whom do you love and trust more? Your God, or your money?

At that, the man's vigor melted more quickly than ice cream on an Arizona sidewalk. The Bible doesn't even record a response from him, just that "he went away sorrowful, for he had great possessions" (Mark 10:22).

This man had built his identity on his wealth and possessions. He had made them his god. When Jesus challenged him to give away his money and prove he truly trusted God, the man walked away sad. Without his possessions, he didn't know who he was; maybe he was even afraid of who he was. Either way, the very thought of leaving his comfort zone terrified him.

Like a match put underneath a running faucet, the flame that had burned so hot only moments earlier was extinguished.

Disappointed, Jesus turned to His disciples.

> Children, how difficult it is to enter the kingdom of God! It is easier for a camel to go through the eye of a needle than for a rich person to enter the kingdom of God. (Mark 10:24–25)

My first inclination upon reading this man's story is to think, "What an idiot."

This man understood Jesus' purpose. He wasn't just another groupie who wanted to join Jesus' entourage in the hope of seeing some cool stuff along the way. He knew Jesus was offering eternal life, and he just threw it away.

But am I so different? Are you?

I'm well aware of God's divinity. I know without a shadow of a doubt that because Jesus sacrificed Himself for me, I'm going to heaven someday. No question.

And yet, like this young man, I'm constantly offered Jesus' hand, and I say, "No, thanks. I'm good."

I'm moved by the radical stories I see and hear, of people donating time every weekend to a local charity, or more, those that move halfway around the world because they feel called by God to witness.

Yet I don't do radical things myself. You're more likely to find me on my couch binging *Top Chef* than changing someone's life.

I tithe my 10 percent, and I'll throw in some extra if my church collects an offering for a particular cause.

Yet I live a comfortable life with good finances, nowhere near the line of sacrificial giving.

I know that heaven is an eternity of worship, blessings, and time with God. One millisecond of heaven far outweighs decades' worth of suffering on earth.

Yet I spend far more time thinking about this life than the one that's coming.

Jesus may not have physically asked me to give all that I have to the poor, but He's asked me to be willing to lose my life for Him. Look at Matthew 16:24–26:

> Then Jesus told His disciples, "If anyone would come after Me, let him deny himself and take up his cross and follow Me. For whoever would save his life will lose it, but whoever loses his life for My sake will find it. For what will it profit a man if he gains the whole

> world and forfeits his soul? Or what shall a man give in return for his soul?"

Jesus' response to the rich young man caused quite a stir among the disciples. If this rock star, this high school quarterback dating the prom queen, can't get into heaven, what chance did a bunch of vagabonds like them stand?

But here's the point we can't miss: Jesus wasn't disappointed with the man because he was rich. The man could have been worth two billion dollars or two cents. Jesus didn't care about that. The only reason He brought up wealth was because that's what the young man valued most.

When push came to shove, he considered his worldly possessions more valuable than the riches awaiting him in heaven.

He was lukewarm.

I don't know you, dear reader, but I'm guessing God isn't asking you to sell all your possessions. He does request that of some people, but they're very few and far between. More likely, He sees something you value more than Him in your life—status, wealth, relationship, self-worth, and so on—and He wants you to give it up.

Look back at the last verse from Matthew: Jesus asks you to deny yourself, take up your cross, and follow Him. Carrying a cross is not a one-handed exercise. It takes one's full concentration and strength. If you're holding onto something else with one hand, you're not budging your cross.

One of two things will happen: you'll keep pushing but not see any movement, or you'll drop your cross and walk away. You'll become lukewarm.

And that's evil.

Like it or not, that's how God sees it. He says so in Malachi 1:8:

> When you offer blind animals in sacrifice, is that not evil? And when you offer those that are lame or sick, is that not evil? Present that to your governor; will he accept you or show you favor? says the LORD of hosts.

Jesus builds on this thought with His parable in Matthew 25:14–30. In the tale, a wealthy man gathered three servants before heading on a trip. After assessing their abilities, he entrusted each with several talents (a talent was a very large amount of money, equal to about twenty years of wages for a common laborer): the first received five; the second, two; and the third, one. The first two servants worked and invested the money, doubling the amount they were given. When their master returned, he was very pleased and regarded them as "good and faithful" servants (verses 21, 23).

Then there's the third servant. Lazy and afraid of failure, he simply buried his talent in the ground. He returned it to his master, pleased that he hadn't lost the money.

But the wealthy man was furious. "You wicked and slothful servant!" he seethed (verse 26):

> You ought to have invested my money with the bankers, and at my coming I should have received what was my own with interest. So take the talent from him and give it to him who has the ten talents. For to everyone who has will more be given, and he will have an abundance. But from the one who has not, even what he has will be taken away. And cast the worthless servant into the outer darkness. In that

> place there will be weeping and gnashing of teeth. (Matthew 25:27–30)

Yikes.

But that's reality. We're all given specific abilities that can help further God's kingdom (1 Corinthians 12). Will we use the skills He gave us to make a difference? Or will we muddle through life, surviving day-to-day, only to hand our talent back to God as is when we arrive at heaven's gates?

Did we really know Jesus? Or did we just know about Him?

Look at Matthew 7:21–23:

> Not everyone who says to Me, "Lord, Lord," will enter the kingdom of heaven, but the one who does the will of My Father who is in heaven. On that day many will say to Me, "Lord, Lord, did we not prophesy in Your name, and cast out demons in Your name, and do many mighty works in Your name?" And then will I declare to them, "I never knew you; depart from Me, you workers of lawlessness."

In sports, athletes that talk a big game but can't back it up with their play are scolded by their peers. "Talk is cheap," their opponents chide. "You just talk the talk, but you can't walk the walk."

This is the problem with lukewarm Christians. They show up for church every Sunday with a friendly smile. They tithe their ten percent. They memorize Scripture. Again, these are all very good practices!

But some masquerade as superstar Christians. And when the fourth quarter arrives and God asks them to stretch their faith, they haven't spent enough time getting to know Him to handle the task.

The lukewarm believer's faith is built like a house of cards—it looks great on the outside, but it's liable to crumble at the first breeze of hardship. It's as Jesus described in Matthew 7:24–27. Those that listen to His teaching and actually put it into action are like a wise man who builds his home on the rock. Even when harsh weather comes, that rock isn't moving. Even with turbulence all around him, that man knows that his foundation is strong. His house is safe.

On the other hand, the man who hears Jesus' teaching and doesn't live it out builds his house on the sand. The first rain washes out the foundation, and that house of cards, that lukewarm structure, comes crashing down.

That's what happened to Solomon.

Solomon

I bet you didn't expect to find Solomon in this chapter, did you? David's heir was the wisest man in history. He penned two books of the Bible and contributed to two others. He oversaw the construction of God's temple in Jerusalem, and his forty-year reign coincided with the most peaceful and prosperous period in Israel's history.

This king was absolutely on fire for God. In fact, he obtained his legendary wisdom because when God offered him anything he wished, the young king asked for "an understanding mind to govern your people, that I may discern between good and evil" (1 Kings 3:9). He combined this intelligence with a love for God (1 Kings 3:3), and God blessed him greatly: "King Solomon excelled all the kings of the earth in riches and in wisdom" (1 Kings 10:23).

That doesn't sound very lukewarm, right?

That's the thing—as long as Solomon kept his focus on God, he was unstoppable. But success loosened his morals, and then things started to go downhill.

When God first established Israel as a nation, He expressly forbade them from marrying people from other nations (Deuteronomy 7:2–4). These relationships would expose the Israelites to pagan religions and lead them away from God.

For all his wisdom, Solomon must have missed that day in Bible class.

The Bible says he "loved many foreign women" (1 Kings 11:1). That's an understatement on the level of saying, "The Cookie Monster from *Sesame Street* mildly enjoys the occasional baked confection." Our hero married seven hundred wives of royal birth and had another three hundred concubines.

Just as God had warned, "his wives turned away his heart" (1 Kings 11:3). He began worshiping other gods, and then he built shrines for them. His lust caused his heart to turn away from God, to the point where God informed him that the kingdom of Israel would be torn from his line (1 Kings 11:11–13).

Even the wisest man in history wasn't immune to Satan's traps. When he diverted his attention from the One who had blessed him, he made some serious mistakes.

Such promise. Such squandered potential.

> Did not Solomon king of Israel sin on account of such women? Among the many nations there was no king like him, and he was beloved by his God, and God made him king over all Israel. Nevertheless, foreign women made even him to sin. (Nehemiah 13:26)

The takeaway from Solomon's life is just as crucial as that from the rich young man. While the rich young man didn't allow his flame to flourish, Solomon caught fire. He obeyed and loved God. He stayed in consistent communication with His Maker and adhered to His teachings. But then Solomon got fat and happy and it all fell apart.

As with the rich young man, this story feels all too familiar to me. Early in his life, Solomon was unproven and tasked with filling the shoes left by David, one of the most revered people in the Bible, as Israel's king. He needed God's guidance and aid to gain his footing. He was an amateur walking a tightrope thirty thousand feet above the ground, and God offered His heavenly hand for assistance.

But once Solomon felt comfortable, he essentially told God, "I got this," and directly disobeyed God's command. He gradually loosened his grip on God's hand until he slipped, and there was nothing to save him from the long fall below.

Similarly, I've had periods of life in which I'm all in on serving God. The Holy Spirit is unleashed in me, free to roam and fill me with God's wisdom and love. I feel as one with God: He's connected to my every thought. I'm more positive. I'm more generous. I love people more.

But I've found these on-fire moments tend to come during times of trial or strife: when I'm struggling at work, when I'm doubting myself, when I feel a relationship crumbling. In those desperate moments, I race to God with arms extended.

When things are going well, though, my passion doesn't burn nearly as bright. One day of missed Bible study turns into two, which extends to a week. My prayers are spurred out of obligation, not love. My comfort lessens my dependence on my Maker.

I don't know why this is. I readily attribute my successes and talents to God. I understand and acknowledge that I'm a mess without Him. Yet my passion doesn't match this knowledge. I feel like a disappointment, which makes me feel unworthy and leads me even farther away from God.

But here's the promising truth: no matter how often you put God in the back seat, He'll never do the same to you. It's important to remember the rich young man's response to Jesus: "*he* became very sad" (Luke 18:23, emphasis added), and "*he* went away sorrowful" (Matthew 19:22, emphasis added). Jesus didn't push him away. He opened His arms and gave the man a chance to change the world.

It was the young man's choice to walk away. He was responsible for his decision.

We never hear from the young man again. It's entirely possible that he realized his error and returned to Christ, but the Bible doesn't comment on him after this point.

But what would have happened if he did change his mind? What if he walked for ten minutes, realized what a terrible mistake he had made, and sprinted to catch back up with Jesus? Out of breath and bent over clutching his knees, he would look up, lock eyes with Jesus, and say, "I'm sorry, Lord. I messed up, but I see clearly now. My life is Yours."

We don't have to speculate on what Jesus' response would be. He demonstrates His stance in the parable of the prodigal son (Luke 15:11–32): open arms, immediate acceptance, and a massive party.

In other words, the opposite of lukewarm.

In fact, Jesus was the opposite of lukewarm in just about every way. I worry that our view of Jesus has become warped by paintings of smiling Jesus with children on His lap and casually sharing the Last Supper with His friends. Sure, Jesus had a gentle side.

He also became so angry that He crafted a whip and drove evildoers out of the temple.

Shortly after Jesus and the apostles arrived in Jerusalem, they visited the temple (John 2:14–16). In the Court of the Gentiles—the outer area that surrounded the inner sacred courts—merchants and money changers had set up booths to take advantage of those who had traveled great distances for Passover. These people were selling sacrificial animals at high prices and deceiving foreigners with high exchange rates for special temple coins. They were using God's house as a way to make money, defiling His home with fraudulent actions.

I'll give you one guess how that sat with Jesus.

Jesus proceeded to weave cords into a whip and chase the merchants out of the temple. He poured out the money changers' coins and upended their tables. If you ever wondered what Jesus would have looked like as the Hulk, this is it.

With money, furniture, and animals splayed out across the court's grounds, Jesus turned to the bewildered remaining evildoers and demanded, "Is it not written, 'My house shall be called a house of prayer for all the nations'? But you have made it a den of robbers" (Mark 11:17).

It's not the way we typically view Jesus, but that's how passionate He was about His mission. In this case, He needed more than stern words and parables to drive His point home. I'm willing to bet the temple never had an issue with commercialism again.

There was no lukewarm in Jesus. His devotion ran scalding hot at all times, and He used different forms to display His zeal.

This is the Man we're called to follow (1 John 2:6; 1 Corinthians 11:1).

Let me leave you with this final (and admittedly odd) analogy: imagine God dining at a restaurant, and your life is the main course. Do you want to serve Him a perfectly cooked, hot burger with crispy bacon and cheese melting down the patty? Or a microwaved, wrinkly brick between buns?

That's what I thought.

CHAPTER 7

Naivete

If any of you lacks wisdom,
let him ask God, who gives generously
to all without reproach, and it will be given him.
(James 1:5)

Of all the jobs I've held, the one that tested me the most was also the most blue-collar: construction worker.

The summer before I left for college, I left my cushy job as a grocery store clerk to work at a concrete and caulking company owned by a member of my church. He needed cheap labor, and I wanted a job with more hours and better wages. I knew the job would be more physically demanding, but I was unprepared for the mental strain that would come from my new position.

The problem was that I always felt like an idiot.

Most of the other people on the crew had been in the industry for years. They knew how to expertly caulk a parking garage, mix concrete, use a jackhammer, and so forth.

I knew none of this. I could barely even figure out how to insert the caulking canister into the dispenser. I was constantly having to ask for direction or help, and my co-workers often had to go back and redo an area I had messed up. There were days when I'm not even sure my presence was a net positive.

For the most part, the other workers were actually very kind to me. They always answered my questions and would walk me through new tasks. A few of them had some choice words for the idiot rookie, but considering how far I was behind everyone else, they treated me with consideration.

But I felt like a burden. In my mind, every question I asked only slowed down the more experienced workers. Every moment spent giving me a tutorial or correcting one of my mistakes took away from time that could have been spent more productively. Though I never really considered quitting, there were days I certainly felt like it. I was so far behind already, so what was the point of trying to catch up?

I think that's how a lot of people feel about Bible class.

Joining a small group or attending a church service can be intimidating, especially for the first time. The unknown is frightening: will you be judged? Will people chuckle at your lack of knowledge? Will you slow down the group if you ask for further explanation?

Sometimes, it feels easier to just back off. Church might be great, but it's for people who grew up in the faith, people who already know what they're doing. People who know the difference between Daniel and Deuteronomy. People who can recite Mark 11:4 and Hebrews 6:15 without blinking.

That's utter nonsense.

I understand why it's a tough mental hurdle to clear, but that feeling of inadequacy is a blatant lie from Satan.

Jesus is for everyone, especially those who are uneducated but passionate to learn more. He even responds to and encourages His enemies.

Just look at Nicodemus.

Nicodemus

To understand Nicodemus's story, we first must dive into the tension that existed between Jesus and the Jewish leaders. Allow me a brief analogy to set the scene.

Imagine you're the longtime owner of the only hardware store in a small town. After years and years of advising customers on home repair and learning about the best tools for every job, you've established a reputation as the community's go-to source for all things hardware. You are extremely well-respected and have a flawless reputation.

Then one day, a new guy saunters into town. He starts handing out home upkeep advice left and right, and many of his philosophies directly clash with yours. Your customers are skeptical but intrigued, and they begin to gravitate toward the newcomer. Nothing you do can get the attention off of this intruder.

That's how the Pharisees felt about Jesus.

As the religious leaders of the day, the Pharisees weren't used to being challenged. The Jewish people admired their dedication and biblical knowledge, so they didn't challenge their authority. The Pharisees were above reproach.

Then Jesus arrived and exposed them. This is where my hardware store analogy needs an additional layer. The Pharisees believed that the Bible's Old Testament was a handbook for how to earn your way to heaven by works. They added their own traditions to make it more clear how to do that. For example, consider the Fourth Commandment: "Remember the Sabbath day, to keep it holy" (Exodus 20:8). The Pharisees counted their steps to ensure they didn't work too much and break the commandment, although that particular directive is never expressed in the Bible. In doing so, they raised themselves up as experts who were better at interpreting God's Word than the common person.

Either no one was brave enough to call them on it, or the people trusted the Pharisees because they didn't know any better. It was as if the hardware shop owner directed customers toward more expensive products or particular brands rather than the best solution.

This caused the Pharisees and Jesus to butt heads again and again from the moment He began teaching. The people were powerless to question the experts. Jesus had no such fear.

One of the best examples of His boldness occurs in Luke 11:37–53. A religious leader invited Jesus to his home for dinner. Jesus declined to wash His hands before the meal. This practice was an Old Testament cleansing that God required only of priests when they were going to perform their work at the temple, but the Pharisees had extended this rule to everyone. The host was incredulous that Jesus rejected this practice, and Jesus noticed his attitude.

> Now you Pharisees cleanse the outside of the cup and of the dish, but inside you are full of greed and wickedness. You fools! Did not He who made the outside make the inside also? (Luke 11:39–40)

Remember, He said this as a dinner guest in a man's home!

Not a timid person, that Jesus.

The real difference between Jesus and the Pharisees was that they believed God had given His Law to show us how to earn a ticket to heaven. Jesus understood that God gave His Law to show us our sin; we need a Savior to get to heaven.

While the Pharisees touted diligence and self-reliance, Jesus promoted repentance and faith.

Needless to say, most of the Pharisees were intimidated and threatened by this newcomer, and they continually looked for ways to expose and undermine Him.

Except one: Nicodemus. Intrigued by this new Teacher, he snuck out to meet Jesus under the cover of night (John 3:1–21).

This was a huge risk. Nicodemus was not only a Pharisee but also a member of the high council, the Sanhedrin. If he was caught fraternizing with the enemy, he could tarnish his reputation and even lose his position.

But there was something different about this Jesus, and Nicodemus decided meeting Him was worth the risk. He even admitted something to Jesus that would have caused his colleagues to gasp aloud:

> Rabbi, we know that You are a teacher come from God, for no one can do these signs that You do unless God is with him. (John 3:2)

Still, while Nicodemus saw Jesus' works and recognized God's hand in His ministry, he had yet to make the connection that Jesus was truly God: "Your miraculous signs are evidence that God is with You."

Rather than greeting the Pharisee, Jesus replied, "Truly, truly, I say to you, unless one is born again he cannot see the kingdom of God" (verse 3). No introductions and pleasantries. That is a heavy statement to begin a conversation.

Jesus' words established the new reality:

- Blood lines and heritage would no longer be the determining factors for who got into heaven.
- God's grace would be available to everyone who was born again, including Gentiles.
- While heaven is a very real place, God's kingdom exists in the hearts of believers, a truth Jesus expanded on in Luke 17:20–21.
- Believers had to be born twice—first with physical birth, then with the waters of Baptism.

Jesus turned Nicodemus' world upside down in a single sentence. The Pharisees believed that they were already right with God thanks to their good works. Jesus turned the tables by enlightening Nicodemus that one must be born again and made a new being by God through Baptism, or heaven was unattainable.

The Pharisee was too taken aback to utter an intelligent response: "How can a man be born when he is old? Can he enter a second time into his mother's womb and be born?" (John 3:4).

Clearly, Jesus wasn't speaking literally. This idea was so revolutionary that I can't blame Nicodemus for momentarily having his brain scrambled. Jesus rocked the cornerstone of his beliefs, and like a boxer who just took a haymaker to the chin, Nicodemus was still woozily regaining his bearings.

But Jesus was just getting started. Over the next seventeen verses, He told Nicodemus that believers must be born again of water and the Spirit through Baptism. Those who are born of the flesh are sinners who will perish, but people born again in Baptism are new creatures bearing the likeness of God. He pointed out the people that had been baptized by John and the radical difference the Holy Spirit was already making in their lives.

Then came the most quoted verse of the Bible, a passage any Christian (and many nonbelievers) can recite by heart, John 3:16:

> For God so loved the world, that He gave His only Son, that whoever believes in Him should not perish but have eternal life.

There's a reason that verse has gained such a foothold. It essentially sums up Jesus' sacrifice and gift to the world. God loved humans so much that He separated Himself from and punished His perfect Son, Jesus, just to give us a chance to live with Him forever. All we have to do is believe in that promise.

It is truly the most lopsided trade-off in history, but God loves us so much, He doesn't care. He doesn't want fair. He wants us.

For all the deserved fanfare John 3:16 receives, the following verse gets slept on in terms of importance. Jesus continued: "For God did not send His Son into the world to condemn the world, but in order that the world might be saved through Him" (verse 17).

From my experiences, the biggest reason nonbelievers resist God is because they view Him as a judge, jury, and executioner. They think He delights in telling them what they can't do and scolding them for their sins. Who would choose to follow a ruler such as that?

But the truth is that God passionately loves us. The rules He created are for our benefit, not to restrict us. He sent Jesus into the world not to condemn us, but to save us!

Nicodemus is a perfect example of this truth. As a Pharisee, he was a part of a hypocritical, corrupt group that focused more on rules than a relationship with God (Mark 2:27), placed unrealistic burdens on the people that they themselves did not keep (Luke 11:45–46), and put on a show to elevate themselves above the common people (Matthew 23:5–7). Anyone who was a part of this club needed a serious realignment of priorities.

But Nicodemus humbly came to Jesus and sought a change. He recognized that the Pharisees might not have everything right and was willing to consider other solutions.

Nicodemus may have had a doctorate in Scripture knowledge, but these verses show how much of a newbie he truly was. It was as if he were entering a church for the first time, not totally sure of what he believed. The next time you feel like a fraud, consider that Jesus called Nicodemus and his peers "blind fools" (Matthew 23:17) and "hypocrites" (Matthew 23:27).

And yet He still accepted Nicodemus. Jesus saw a student who was earnest and eager to learn. His past behavior wasn't acceptable, but Nicodemus showed he was willing to change. Jesus taught him. Notice that He didn't use dumbed-down language. He presented Nicodemus with life-altering knowledge and challenged him to believe.

Jesus' words caused Nicodemus to recognize he was in the wrong and begin to move in the right direction. At the Feast of Booths, Jesus spoke to the crowd:

> If anyone thirsts, let him come to Me and drink.
> Whoever believes in Me, as the Scripture has said,
> "Out of his heart will flow rivers of living water."
> (John 7:37–38)

This threatened the Pharisees' laws, but the temple guards were so awed they declined to arrest Jesus. When the Pharisees questioned their resistance, Nicodemus replied, "Does our law judge a man without first giving him a hearing and learning what he does?" (John 7:51).

This was a bold move by Nicodemus. It was unheard of for a Pharisee to defend Jesus in any way. He risked—and received—serious judgment from his peers. Immediately, they began to question and discredit him, but Nicodemus didn't back down.

After Jesus was crucified, Joseph (not Jesus' father, but another by the same name), asked Pilate for permission to bury Jesus' body in a tomb he owned. And Nicodemus brought seventy-five pounds of perfumed ointments to help preserve and honor His body (John 19:39).

While his peers rejected and crucified Jesus, Nicodemus finally stood up to them and honored the Man he recognized as his Savior. Nicodemus was willing to differentiate himself publicly from the other Pharisees and say, "This is my God, my Savior, and my friend."

And Jesus loved him.

As a Pharisee, Nicodemus had an extensive religious background. But in many ways, he was as blind as any Gentile. He didn't really understand Jesus' mission or what He was all about. For everything Nicodemus thought he knew, he didn't even really understand the Old Testament.

But Nicodemus was willing to learn.

He humbled himself and came before this Man he didn't know. He did so in secret at first, afraid of judgment from his peers. But as he learned more and more about Jesus, he became assured that loving Jesus wasn't about intellectual knowledge. It was about love:

Jesus' love for him, and his loving response. Over time, he grew bold enough to challenge and even defy his peers in defense of his God.

On the opposite end of the knowledge spectrum was Zacchaeus, a man whose biblical education was likely even shorter than his diminutive height. Yet Jesus' response to his curiosity speaks volumes.

ZACCHAEUS

Late in Jesus' ministry, He and the disciples passed through Jericho on the way to Jerusalem. As usual, Jesus' appearance caused quite a stir, and rumors of this miracle worker's arrival brought out droves of inquisitive onlookers. They wanted to be healed, hear one of His famed sermons, or simply see Him.

Among the crowd was a tax collector named Zacchaeus (Luke 19). He had heard about this Jesus, a celebrity who not only accepted but embraced tax collectors such as himself; in fact, one of His twelve disciples (Matthew) was a former tax collector (Matthew 9:9–13). Most people rejected Zacchaeus because of his profession, and now there was this miracle worker who associated and dined with sinners? This he had to see!

The problem was that Zacchaeus was a bit, well, height-challenged. He had no chance at seeing Jesus in a crowd "because he was small in stature" (Luke 19:3).

What he lacked in size, he made up for in ingenuity. Zacchaeus wouldn't be denied this once-in-a-lifetime opportunity to see Jesus, so he climbed a sycamore tree that was along Jesus' upcoming path and waited to catch a glimpse of this superstar.

While I can't say for certain that Zacchaeus didn't have faith, what little details the Bible gives us about his life suggests he wasn't following religious laws too closely. We know a few things about Zacchaeus:

1. He was the chief tax collector of the region. To keep the wheels of their great empire churning, the Romans levied heavy taxes on the Jewish people. The Jews despised this, as they were forced to support a secular government. Tax collectors were among the most unpopular people of that time.
2. He held this position despite being a Jew, meaning that he prioritized his bank account over his morals and his brethren.
3. He cheated the people and kept extra money for himself. The people referred to him as a sinner (Luke 19:7), and he admitted to defrauding people (Luke 19:8).

Zacchaeus turned his back on his people—Jesus' people—and cheated them for personal gain. He doesn't seem like the type Jesus would befriend, right?

Yet when Jesus saw Zacchaeus perched in the tree, He called out to him: "Zacchaeus, hurry and come down, for I must stay at your house today" (Luke 19:5). Not only did Jesus know Zacchaeus' name, but He also wanted to spend time with and get to know this man.

Zacchaeus climbed down and joyfully welcomed Jesus into his home. He offered to give half his wealth to the poor and pay back four times the amount he had cheated people on their taxes.

There was a zeal to Zacchaeus that we can't miss. Given his prior actions, he didn't know much about God, or he just outright ignored God's teachings. When he climbed the tree, Zacchaeus was the person sneaking into the last row of the sanctuary five minutes after the service started—curious and willing to learn, but ashamed of himself and willing only to witness Jesus from afar, with a quick exit strategy if necessary.

But Jesus completely accepted this sinner. Jesus didn't care what Zacchaeus had done or what the crowd thought of him. He risked His reputation to spend time with Zacchaeus.

And you know what? It was worth it.

> Today salvation has come to this house, since he also is a son of Abraham. For the Son of Man came to seek and to save the lost. (Luke 19:9–10)

Jesus didn't care that Zacchaeus was a little rough around the edges. He didn't care that he was a liar, or that he cheated his own people.

He didn't care that Zacchaeus wasn't a biblical scholar.

He cared that he cared.

Jesus was more interested in Zacchaeus than He was in any of the Pharisees who could recite the entire Old Testament. They seemed to have all the biblical knowledge in the world, but they actually missed the Book's entire point. The Pharisees viewed the Bible as a rulebook for earning one's way to heaven, failing to understand it was about the coming Savior—Jesus Christ, now walking among them.

While they looked impressive and worthy of respect in human eyes, Jesus warned about listening to teachers who didn't understand what they were saying:

> The scribes and the Pharisees sit on Moses' seat, so do and observe whatever they tell you, but not the works they do. For they preach, but do not practice. (Matthew 23:2–3)

> Beware of the scribes, who like to walk around in long robes, and love greetings in the marketplaces and the best seats in the synagogues and the places of honor at feasts, who devour widows' houses and for a pretense make long prayers. They will receive the greater condemnation. (Luke 20:46–47)

The Pharisees put on a great show. They closely followed rituals and presented impressive-sounding prayers. But their actions and words were hollow.

> So also faith by itself, if it does not have works, is dead. (James 2:17)

That's why Jesus, who was constantly at odds with the religious leaders, was so excited to dine with Zacchaeus. This man didn't have knowledge, but he had passion. He wanted—needed—to learn, while all the Pharisees wanted to do was prove their superiority.

Ultimately, I think that's why the other workers at the job site put up with me (other than the fact that they were just good people). For my naivete, I was a hard worker who stayed until the job was done, not when the clock hit 5:00 p.m. My mishaps left me with a series of cuts and bruises, but I always showed up the next morning. My dedication and attendance earned their respect. Over time, as I learned more and got some practice, I started making contributions (still minimal, but it was something).

So it is with most churches and Bible studies. Not all are perfect, and I'm willing to bet anyone reading this has had a bad experience or two. But I've found that if Christians really revere God and love with brotherly affection (Romans 12:10), they're open and inviting to all, especially those that don't know much.

While Nicodemus and Zacchaeus are vastly different people, they share a few common traits: they recognized Jesus' divinity, they acknowledged He had something they didn't, and they were willing to go to great lengths to learn more about Him.

Whether you're completely new to the faith or have gone to church your whole life but are wrestling with the feeling that there's something more, just come to Jesus. Get involved at church. Read the Bible. Pray to Him. He doesn't care what you say. He just wants to hear you and teach you about His Father's grace and boundless love.

In other words, just keep showing up to the job site. You're not a nuisance.

You're beloved.

Matthew 7:7 puts a perfect bow on this chapter:

> Ask, and it will be given to you; seek, and you will find; knock, and it will be opened to you.

CHAPTER 8

Pride

But far be it from me to boast except in the cross of our Lord Jesus Christ, by which the world has been crucified to me, and I to the world. (Galatians 6:14)

In the summer of 2020, I was riding high—perhaps a little too high.

Because (now, don't laugh), I was kind of the "Omaha food guy."

I don't hide from my status as an avid foodie. In fact, I'm so passionate about promoting locally-owned restaurants around my hometown of Omaha, Nebraska, that I started a website with restaurant reviews and dining suggestions. Over time, I became a trusted resource for Omaha diners.

I had more than ten thousand followers on Twitter that regularly consulted me on where to eat and sent me pictures of their meals from restaurants I recommended. I was one of the most prominent members of an Omaha Food Lovers Facebook group, where my thoughts held real sway with the masses. My website received hundreds of visits each day. I even went on a few local radio shows to talk about the best eats around Omaha.

But more than anything, I had my podcast.

Late in 2019, I started recording *Restaurant Hoppen* at a local studio. The first episodes mostly consisted of me shooting the breeze about burgers and restaurant news with my friends and local media members. It was more fun than anything else.

Then the chefs and owners of Block 16, my favorite restaurant, agreed to come on the show. Not only were Jessica Joyce Urban and Paul Urban fantastic guests, but they're also heavy hitters in the Omaha food scene. Their appearance gave *Restaurant Hoppen* legitimacy and gave me respect among the very chefs I so admired.

Now I found when I invited chefs and restaurateurs on the show, they were eager to accept, and as the show continued to grow, they even began asking to appear. Suddenly, I had more than a cult following. I had a strong voice and a platform to help shine a light on deserving, hard-working people and their great restaurants.

The only thing growing faster than my reputation was the size of my head. And that was a problem.

God has given me a great ability to interview. I've been told I have a way of putting people at ease. Most of my guests were unfamiliar with the interview setting and instinctually began the episode guarded and unsure of themselves. But my low-key nature and follow-up questions allowed me to help my guests loosen up. This created great conversation and, in turn, great podcasts.

This skill is a blessing, but I lost sight of its source. As more praise and notoriety came my way, I inhaled it like a vacuum. I believed that *Restaurant Hoppen* was the product of my own hard work and success. That was true to an extent, but I began to push God out of the spotlight, and I needed to be woken up to face reality.

Of all the sins God disapproves of, I feel pride is pretty close to the top of the list. I'll list just a few verses that provide a window into how He feels about it:

> Thus says the Lord: "Let not the wise man boast in his wisdom, let not the mighty man boast in his might, let not the rich man boast in his riches." (Jeremiah 9:23)

> Do nothing from selfish ambition or conceit, but in humility count others more significant than yourselves. (Philippians 2:3)

> Pride goes before destruction, and a haughty spirit before a fall. (Proverbs 16:18)

> By insolence comes nothing but strife, but with those who take advice is wisdom. (Proverbs 13:10)

And just in case it's not crystal clear yet:

> Everyone who is arrogant in heart is an abomination to the Lord; be assured, he will not go unpunished. (Proverbs 16:5)

Not a lot of gray area, is there? God hates pride. Ego and self-love pave the highway to destruction.

Samson

Samson is a prime example of pride in the Bible.

Few people in history were blessed with Samson's physical attributes. A judge whom God appointed to lead the Israelites while they were under Philistine rule, Samson was granted tremendous physical strength and ability in battle. This man massacred a thousand Philistines in one day with the jawbone of a donkey (Judges 15:15), escaped capture by removing a town's gates (Judges 16:3), and killed a lion by ripping it apart with his bare hands (Judges 14:6).

Needless to say, this is the kind of person you want on your side in a fight. Samson was an incredible warrior, a one-man wrecking crew that caused battle-hardened soldiers to soil themselves.

Unfortunately, he forgot his strength came from the Holy Spirit, not himself.

Samson's arrogance leaps off the Bible's pages. God's Law expressly forbids His people from marrying people of enemy tribes (Exodus 34:16; Deuteronomy 7:1–4), but Samson, upon spotting a pretty young Philistine woman, went home and told his parents, "I saw one of the daughters of the Philistines at Timnah. Now get her for me as my wife" (Judges 14:2).

That woman later became his wife; that is, until the father gave her to Samson's best man (now that's cold). Understandably peeved, Samson responded by setting fire in the Philistine fields. The men of Judah, fearful of the Philistine retaliation, cautiously came to arrest him and hand him over to their enemies.

Samson's response? No problem. "Swear to me that you will not attack me yourselves" (Judges 15:12). He then proceeded to break free and unleash the aforementioned jawbone slaughter.

He carried on a clearly toxic relationship with a different Philistine girlfriend despite all kinds of warning flags. Multiple times, Delilah (upon a bribe from the Philistines) asked Samson about the source of his strength and what it would take to tie him up securely (Judges 16:6, 10, 13, 15–16). Each time, she bound him in his sleep with his latest suggestion. Then Philistine soldiers came to arrest him, and Samson (who had lied) snapped out of his bonds and defeated his enemies with ease.

Why carry on this clearly paper-thin relationship? Samson found Delilah attractive, and he didn't think she posed any real threat. What were a few bowstrings and some measly Philistine soldiers? The benefits that came with this relationship far outweighed the minimal effort it took for him to dispose of his enemies.

Samson's problem was that he had no fear.

Because he never failed, he felt invincible, without any need of help. I find it quite telling that out of everything we're told of Samson's life in the Bible, we find only two prayers. The first was a complaint (we'll get to the second soon):

> And he was very thirsty, and he called upon the LORD and said, "You have granted this great salvation by the hand of Your servant, and shall I now die of thirst and fall into the hands of the uncircumcised?" (Judges 15:18)

This gripe comes on the heels of Samson's jawbone slaughter. As the Israelites handed the bound Samson over to his enemies, "The Spirit of the LORD rushed upon him" (Judges 15:14), allowing him to snap the ropes and exact his revenge.

In fact, you can look back at nearly every awesome act Samson performed and find some variation of that phrase (Judges 14:6, 19). Samson's power never came from his own strength; it was always from God.

During all Samson's tales of conquest, the spotlight never shifts off him and onto the One who deserved the praise. As Samson soaked in the glory, his ego grew until he felt untouchable.

I bet you can relate.

No, you've probably never rampaged through bloody battle over your enemies or conquered a lion. But we all go through hot streaks in life. Everything is going well at work. Your relationships are all lined up. You look in the mirror and see your new diet and workout routine are paying dividends.

What happens to your prayer life during a hot streak?

I don't know about you, but the more comfortable I get, the less I tend to lean on God. I start reading my own headlines and believing I'm the source of my success.

That's a good way to get humbled really quickly, as Samson found out.

Samson was a Nazirite, meaning he was consecrated to God and abstained from drinking alcohol and cutting his hair. In Samson's case, the source of his power was indicated by his flowing locks (Judges 16:17), a fact he eventually confessed to Delilah out of arrogance and desire.

Oops.

While Samson slept, Delilah gave him a haircut, then called in the guards. Samson jolted awake, ready to dispense easily of the pitiful Philistine warriors yet again. But this time his strength was gone, and his enemies captured him and gouged out his eyes.

The mighty warrior was humbled.

This brings us to Samson's second recorded prayer.

The Philistines threw a great party to celebrate the capture of their tormentor. More than three thousand of the most powerful Philistines gathered to revel and drunkenly mock Samson, who was chained to the main pillars of the structure. Despite his perilous situation, Samson sniffed opportunity—but success would require a trait he hadn't tapped into in quite some time.

Humility.

Placing his hands upon the supporting pillars, Samson reached out to God in desperation: "O Lord God, please remember me and please strengthen me only this once, O God, that I may be avenged on the Philistines for my two eyes" (Judges 16:28).

This was the big moment. For years and years, Samson had piled up victories without attributing them to the source. The only reason he changed his tune was his desperate situation.

Would God punish him for this arrogance? Or would He come powerfully upon him to aid him one last time?

As Samson pushed, the gigantic supports buckled like toothpicks, and the roof crushed everyone in attendance.

It took until his final breaths, but Samson finally got it. Life isn't about scoring victories and basking in the limelight. It's about using achievements to point others to God, humbly admitting that without Him we are nothing.

Only with Him do we have true power.

> But He gives more grace. Therefore it says, "God opposes the proud but gives grace to the humble." (James 4:6)

> Toward the scorners He is scornful, but to the humble He gives favor. (Proverbs 3:34)

> "Let the one who boasts, boast in the Lord." For it is not the one who commends himself who is approved, but the one whom the Lord commends. (2 Corinthians 10:17–18)

No matter how much Samson gloated, God never said, "Okay, enough is enough." Samson may have been an egomaniac, but that didn't separate him from God's love.

I find it fascinating to examine the parallels between Samson and Jesus. Consider:

- Both were set apart to work in God's kingdom; Samson as a judge, and Jesus as the Christ.
- Both were filled with and empowered by the Holy Spirit.
- Both performed incredible miracles.
- Both delivered Israel without raising massive armies.
- Both achieved great things in death—Samson essentially crushed the entire Philistine government, while Jesus mortally wounded Satan as He conquered sin, death, and hell.

Of course, there are some dramatic differences too:

- Samson used his miraculous powers for himself and his glory, while Jesus used His exclusively for others.
- Samson was selfish and disobeyed God's Law, while Jesus was selfless and perfectly obedient.
- Samson died as a captive who finally learned to recognize and call on God's power, while Jesus willingly offered Himself up as a sacrifice for us.

It's obviously hyperbole to suggest Samson could have accomplished as much as Jesus; no human can. But it's hard not to look at all the potential with which God presented him and wonder how much more he could have achieved with a shot of humility.

Of course, Samson wasn't the only biblical character to suffer from an inflated ego.

James and John

The brothers James and John were the dynamic duo of Jesus' disciples. Along with Peter, they represented Jesus' inner circle.

John, "whom Jesus loved" (John 13:23), was the only one of the Twelve to stand at Jesus' crucifixion (John 19:26–27). He also penned five books of the Bible. James was the first of the disciples to die for his faith (Acts 12:2).

These were two influential men whom Jesus trusted, but they needed an injection of humility.

Near the end of Jesus' ministry, James and John approached Jesus with their mother. In that day, the Jews expected Jesus would set up His kingdom on earth. Kneeling before Him, she requested that when Jesus established His earthly kingdom, her boys would sit on either side of Him (Matthew 20:20–28).

This was no small request. She basically requested that James and John be placed at the positions of highest honor. Keep in mind, Jesus Himself was to sit at the right hand of God:

> Being therefore exalted at the right hand of God, and having received from the Father the promise of the Holy Spirit, He has poured out this that you yourselves are seeing and hearing. (Acts 2:33)

> The Lord says to my Lord: "Sit at My right hand, until I make your enemies your footstool." (Psalm 110:1)

Making such an audacious request is pure hubris. I also find it a bit comical that James and John, supposedly worthy of being Jesus' closest companions, had to have their mom make their request for them.

Jesus, knowing that He would soon be arrested and crucified, answered, "You do not know what you are asking. Are you able to drink the cup that I am to drink?" (Matthew 20:22).

James and John said to Him, "We are able" (verse 22).

Jesus' bitter cup was the suffering and crucifixion He was about to endure (Matthew 26:39, 42). James and John weren't capable of drinking from that cup—no other person was! But in their pride, they both blindly confirmed they were up to the task, even though they didn't even know what the task was (Mark 9:30–32).

Not only were James and John not ready for or worthy of the position they requested, but they also should have known not to ask for it in the first place. It was as if a scrawny freshman approached the head varsity football coach on game day and said, "I'm starting at middle linebacker tonight, right?"

Jesus' response was twofold. First, He showed the humility that eluded His friends: "But to sit at My right hand and at My left is not Mine to grant, but it is for those for whom it has been prepared by My Father" (Matthew 20:23). He acknowledged that God was in control, not Him. The very position they sought was in fact not His to give out.

Then He continued, "But whoever would be great among you must be your servant, and whoever would be first among you must be your slave, even as the Son of Man came not to be served but to serve, and to give His life as a ransom for many" (verses 26–28).

The reversal of the situation is so stark. As James and John arrogantly requested this position of honor, Jesus was in the process of humbly sacrificing Himself for their sins. In just a short time, He'd be in a tomb as atonement for humanity's fall.

Jesus drove the point home again a few chapters later, as He chastised the haughty religious leaders: "Whoever exalts himself will be humbled, and whoever humbles himself will be exalted" (Matthew 23:12).

His words didn't exactly take hold.

A short time later, Jesus and the disciples shared the Last Supper. Mere hours before His arrest, some of them started arguing about who was the greatest among them (Luke 22:24). I'm willing to bet our brothers didn't sit this debate out.

Jesus' response:

> The kings of the Gentiles exercise lordship over them, and those in authority over them are called benefactors. But not so with you. Rather, let the greatest among you become as the youngest, and the leader as one who serves. For who is the greater, one who reclines at table or one who serves? Is it not the one who reclines at table? But I am among you as the one who serves.
>
> You are those who have stayed with Me in My trials, and I assign to you, as My Father assigned to Me, a kingdom, that you may eat and drink at My table in My kingdom and sit on thrones judging the twelve tribes of Israel. (Luke 22:25–30)

Rather than call out their childish ways, Jesus promised them a kingdom.

But, just as Samson was humbled to learn his lesson, so would the disciples be. They would soon be scattered and left to hide behind locked doors, frightened and unsure of the future. Even after receiving the Holy Spirit (Acts 2:2–4), they would all be arrested and (except for John) killed for preaching the Gospel.

But they had learned their lesson by that point. No longer were they asking for seats alongside Jesus. Rather, they befriended beggars, the crippled, and the diseased. They found humility and freedom at the same time.

Had they looked a bit closer at their leader, they could have learned the value of humility a lot sooner.

Jesus performed a lot of miracles throughout His ministry. These works inspired great admiration and celebration from the people. They spread their cloaks on the ground in front of Him upon His arrival to Jerusalem (Matthew 21:8–9). Large crowds followed Him (Matthew 8:1; 12:15), much like fans crowding the red carpet at a blockbuster movie premiere.

If Jesus wanted to be a superstar, the stage was set for Him.

But He had little interest in human praise. Look at Matthew 9:27–31, in which Jesus heals a pair of blind men. They were astonished when their sight returned. But "Jesus sternly warned them, 'See that no one knows about it'" (Matthew 9:30).

Sternly sounds like a father warning his children, "Listen to me very carefully."

Of course, the men couldn't hold back. They told everyone they knew, and Jesus' fame spread.

Samson would have basked in this limelight, and maybe scheduled a few autograph sessions. James and John would have hired a publicist.

Not Jesus.

Multiple times, He healed people and commanded that they keep quiet. A few other examples:

> And [the deaf man's] ears were opened, his tongue was released, and he spoke plainly. And Jesus charged them to tell no one. But the more He charged them, the more zealously they proclaimed it. (Mark 7:35–36)

> And all were weeping and mourning for her, but He said, "Do not weep, for she is not dead but sleeping." And they laughed at Him, knowing that she was dead. But taking her by the hand He called, saying, "Child, arise." And her spirit returned, and she got up at once. And He directed that something should be given her to eat. And her parents were amazed, but He charged them to tell no one what had happened. (Luke 8:52–56)

Jesus didn't want the spotlight for His miracles. He just wanted to help people.

The only pride He carried was tied to His love and devotion to His Father.

> Jesus answered, "If I glorify Myself, My glory is nothing. It is My Father who glorifies Me, of whom you say, 'He is our God.'" (John 8:54)

The Son of God, the only human who ever earned the right to take pride in Himself and His actions, wanted nothing to do with it. "For everyone who exalts himself will be humbled, but the one who humbles himself will be exalted," He said in Luke 18:14.

Pride causes us to think we don't need God. We become dependent on ourselves and trust in our judgment and abilities.

This begs the question: whom do you trust more, an all-powerful God who created the universe and conquered death itself? Or your flawed human abilities?

(If you answered the latter, I suggest you take a hard look in the mirror and reconsider.)

Let's circle back to my podcast, in which I had taken too much pride. I needed some humbling.

The studio at which I recorded was incredibly reliable, with an ace editor who knew more about audio equipment than anyone I've ever met. In eight months of podcasting, I hadn't had a single issue.

Then I lost my next two podcasts. The audio files vanished into thin air, to the bafflement not only of my producer but also the company that made the recording equipment. The files were garbled and unrecoverable.

Hoping these misfortunes were a coincidence, Sarah and I tried recording a podcast with my own equipment at home. The audio was scratchy and unusable. The same thing happened when I interviewed a guest in a local restaurant a few days later.

To recap: I recorded four episodes in the span of a week. In three different locations. On two devices. And I lost them all.

I'm not saying that God destroyed the podcasts. I don't believe He is vindictive, and it could have just been an unfortunate coincidence.

But those failures caused me to take a step back and look at the situation in a new light. What if God were sending me a message?

Not a threat, but a friendly reminder, a tap on the shoulder, that He's the one with the power. My successes are really His.

It at least made me pause and approach my so-called status a bit differently moving forward. I reminded myself that my podcast was to highlight local restaurants and owners, not myself. They were the ones putting in the hard work. I was only a guy with a microphone.

Amazing what a little perspective can do.

Thankfully, I didn't have to have my eyes gouged out or see my mentor crucified to learn my lesson. But I accepted God's message, and now I know what restaurant to recommend for some humble pie.

CHAPTER 9

Rebelliousness

If one turns away his ear from hearing
the law, even his prayer is an abomination. (Proverbs 28:9)

It's fascinating to me how the ideal of the rebel has been glorified in film. Consider these beloved rebellious figures:

- Ferris Bueller (*Ferris Bueller's Day Off*): a class-cutting thrill-seeker who won our hearts by thumbing his nose at his school principal, parents, and anyone else who stood in the way of him having fun.
- Han Solo (*Star Wars*): a wise-cracking smuggler who inspires with his smooth-talking and exceptional piloting skills.
- Katniss Everdeen (*The Hunger Games*): a no-nonsense heroine whose skill with a bow is matched only by her hard-nosed attitude and desire to overthrow the evil Capitol.
- William Wallace (*Braveheart*): an unstoppable warrior

> whose broadsword cuts down countless English soldiers in an effort to help Scotland gain independence. (Yes, he was also a real person, but would you know of him if not for the movie?)

We love an individual (or group) who is willing to stand up and challenge authority. We treasure their boldness and valor; for that matter, America was built by rebels who were fed up with oppressive British rule.

It's true that a rebel can sometimes be worthy of admiration. Though their causes aren't always virtuous, many rebels take an honorable stand against oppressive forces or rulers, rising up when others are too afraid or powerless to help themselves.

Sounds noble and just, right?

But what happens when the authority is God?

That's when rebellion transforms from an honorable cause into folly. Rebelling against an oppressive, overbearing force is worthy of tales and song; rebelling against our Creator who loved us enough to die for us is just plain stupid.

Why would you ever defy someone described in terms such as these?

- "Their help and your shield" (Psalm 115:11)
- "My light and my salvation" (Psalm 27:1)
- "A very present help in trouble" (Psalm 46:1)
- "My rock and my fortress and my deliverer" (2 Samuel 22:2)

That's someone I want to fight for, not against.

So why do we constantly rebel against God?

It's an incriminating thought that humbles me daily. God is my

Savior. He gave me life and delighted in creating me. He sent His Son to take my place on the cross. He enriches my soul through the Holy Spirit.

Then temptations arise, and I pursue them like a six-year-old chasing down an ice cream truck. Many times, I'm actively aware that I'm breaking God's laws (which He put in place to enhance my life, not hinder it).

And yet I rebel.

To understand why, I think we need to take a look at humanity's first rebels.

Adam and Eve

There are few stories more beautiful than that of creation. God spent six days creating absolutely everything: heavens and earth, sky and sea, day and night, beast and birds. Yet for all these miraculous things He accomplished, His work wasn't done until He created humankind. Only then did He think His work was "very good" (Genesis 1:31).

He didn't conceive of humanity as He did everything else. All of creation was born of God's creativity, but He saved something special for us:

> Then God said, "Let us make man in our image, after our likeness. And let them have dominion over the fish of the sea and over the birds of the heavens and over the livestock and over all the earth and over every creeping thing that creeps on earth."
>
> So God created man in His own image, in the image of God He created him; male and female He created them. (Genesis 1:26–27)

I want you to stop reading for a second. Put down the book if you have to. We have to take a minute to ponder how incredible this is.

Of the trillions of things God created, He only patterned one species after Himself.

You and me.

Seriously, stop and think about that! The all-powerful God of the universe, the One who could destroy everything with a snap of His fingers if He chose, wanted to reflect His nature in you.

The love displayed in that one move is unlike anything you and I can even wrap our tiny human minds around.

And it gets better.

Think of all the incredible animals out there. Can you imagine any other beast besting a healthy lion? How about another fish conquering a great white shark, or a lesser bird taking down a majestic bald eagle?

And yet God gave humankind dominion over these creatures that could so easily overpower us. And He did it with joy.

> Be fruitful and multiply and fill the earth and subdue it, and have dominion over the fish of the sea and over the birds of the heavens and over every living thing that moves on the earth. (Genesis 1:28)

This was the world Adam came into: one of love and nothing else.

I love to picture the first time Adam gained consciousness. As the first human awakes and tries to gain his bearings, God can barely contain His excitement: "Hey, you're up! Welcome to earth! I have so much to show you; we don't have a minute to waste! Come on!"

Their relationship was wonderful, but God recognized that Adam felt alone as the only human. God loved Adam so much that He created a woman, Eve, to serve as Adam's companion (Genesis 2:18–23).

Every step of the way, God did everything, through love, to accommodate this man. With all these blessings came one simple stipulation: don't eat the fruit from the tree of the knowledge of good and evil (Genesis 2:16–17).

The Garden of Eden—the paradise in which Adam lived—was filled with all kinds of wonderful, fruit-bearing plants. From a hunger standpoint, Adam never would have had to resort to eating from the forbidden tree in the center of the garden.

And yet, all it took was the slightest temptation for Adam and Eve to slip up and spoil the paradise God had prepared for them.

A cunning serpent approached Eve and tempted her to eat from the taboo tree. Remembering God's command, Eve was fearful that doing so would kill her. The serpent lied: "You will not surely die. For God knows that when you eat of it your eyes will be opened, and you will be like God, knowing good and evil" (Genesis 3:4–5).

Before we look into how Adam and Eve reacted, let's take a step back. Why did God even put the tree there in the first place? If He loved Adam and Eve so much, why introduce something that could cause His beloved humans to stumble?

That's the amazing thing about God: He gives us the free will to rebel.

From our perspective, the logical solution would have been never to plant the forbidden tree. He could have just created a utopia in which He catered to Adam and Eve's every need, thus retaining their affection.

But that's not friendship. It's not a relationship.

It's not love.

By His very nature, God is love (1 John 4:8, 16). He doesn't desire a mindless following that just worships Him because He treated them well.

Recall my story about my dog, Eve, back in chapter 5, "Impatience." That dog and I had a terrible relationship. She had zero interest in pleasing me; that is, until I produced a treat. Once that little morsel came out of my pocket, Eve would do just about whatever I wanted. She didn't respect me, but she'd put up with me momentarily for this reward.

That's the exact opposite of how God desires us to feel about Him. He loves us so much, and He desires our hearts (Proverbs 23:26). But He won't just keep feeding us treats (blessings) in order to win our allegiance momentarily. He desires a real relationship.

So He plants forbidden trees in our lives and gives us a choice. When we choose Him, we reflect the love that He so graciously shows us.

These temptations look different to everyone. For some, God's tree might be improper sexuality, such as pornography or illicit sexual desires. For others, it is the love of money. Some thirst after fame and status. Examine your heart. You know what your forbidden trees are.

For Adam and Eve, that tree was the knowledge of good and evil. All this pair had known was paradise, and they were curious to explore the depths of God's knowledge that they thought He might be shielding from them.

Eve took a bite from the fruit, and Adam followed suit.

Immediately, their eyes were opened. For the first time, humans felt negative emotions: fear, shame, guilt, embarrassment. God had protected the pair from these things before, but now they flooded Adam's and Eve's minds.

Previously, they had sauntered around Eden in the nude; they felt no shame, so there was no need for clothes. Now they desperately covered themselves with fig branches and looked for a place to hide from God during His daily stroll through the garden.

This is, I fear, frequently my response when I indulge and eat from my forbidden trees. I know in my mind that when I give in to my temptations and sin, my first response should be to return to God, to pray and get into the Word. Only there can I find the answers to help me resist the temptation in the future; more importantly, only there do I find the forgiveness my soul needs.

But all too often, I find myself going in the opposite direction. Just as Adam and Eve hid from their Friend, I resist prayer. Who am I, this dirty, flawed sinner who gives in to simple temptations, to speak with my almighty God? Not only am I unworthy of His presence, but I'm also fearful of the judgment and punishment that approaching Him might bring.

So, like Adam and Eve, I hide.

How stupid.

How is one supposed to hide from a God who can see not only everything happening in the moment (Proverbs 15:3) but also what's happened in the past and will happen in the future (Psalm 139:16)? He even knows what you're thinking right now (1 Chronicles 28:9).

Good luck hiding from Him.

Adam and Eve quickly realized their folly, as God found them rather easily. He asked them, "What is this that you have done?" (Genesis 3:13).

I fear that we read this response as judgment, the all-powerful God belittling and scolding the puny humans, raking them across the coals for their stupidity.

But I see it differently. I see God, ripped apart inside by this betrayal, sinking to His knees and asking in a sorrowful voice: "What have you done? How could you do this to Me?"

"I gave you everything. I love you so much. Why?"

Just thinking of the pain He felt in that moment is gut-wrenching. Despite all the love God showed Adam and Eve, they couldn't resist the one test He presented them.

As a consequence, Adam and Eve were banned from Eden. Eve's choice ensured all women would undergo painful childbirth (Genesis 3:16), while Adam's willingness to join in assured humanity the struggle of growing their own food, rather than relying on God to do so (Genesis 3:17–19).

While that might seem harsh for one mistake, it's actually an incredible display of mercy. Remember God's original instructions to Adam: "For in the day that you eat of it you shall surely die" (Genesis 2:17).

That punishment seems pretty black-and-white. Yet, while Adam and Eve died spiritually on that day (thus needing God's promise of a Savior to be born again, as Jesus later taught Nicodemus), they were allowed to live and be the father and mother of humanity.

What mercy. God had every right to incinerate Adam and Eve in that moment. He warned them. They didn't care. They thumbed their noses in His face and did what they wanted.

Yet God didn't destroy them. He gave them a shot at redemption.

But remember that God is a just God (Ecclesiastes 3:17). Just because He loves you doesn't mean you get to walk all over Him. When you disobey His commands, punishment may very well follow.

But your sins are no longer damning.

Want proof? Just look at Barabbas.

Barabbas

When Jesus was taken before Pilate to be tried under Roman law, a man named Barabbas sat in prison. Unlike Jesus, Barabbas very much earned his incarceration. He had been arrested for starting a violent uprising and murder (Luke 23:19). The Bible tells us very little about this man, but the limited text makes it clear: Barabbas was a rebel in every sense of the word.

The same qualities that made Barabbas a threat to the Roman government made him a hero to many of the Jews. The Jewish people hated their position under the Roman thumb; they were a fiercely independent people who despised paying taxes to support the Roman government and religion. Barabbas's actions, though violent, were viewed by many as heroic.

We'll get back to Barabbas in a minute. Let's set the scene first.

After Jesus was arrested in the Garden of Gethsemane, the Jewish religious leaders quickly put their treacherous plan in motion. They brought Jesus before the high council and hired witnesses to give false testimony against Jesus. "The high priest asked Him, 'Are You the Christ, the Son of the Blessed?' And Jesus said, 'I am, and you will see the Son of Man seated at the right hand of Power, and coming with the clouds of heaven'" (Mark 14:61–62).

That was all the council needed. They were searching for any reason, no matter how flimsy, to incriminate Jesus. In their eyes, He had now committed blasphemy, a sin punishable by death. Though Jesus was telling the truth, the council had their evidence.

But executing Jesus wasn't that simple. Because the Jews were under Roman occupation, they had to get permission to inflict capital punishment. The Jewish ruling body needed Pilate, the Roman governor, to condemn Jesus.

In this lay the Jews' problem: as we discussed in chapter 4, "Fear," Pilate didn't have a problem with Jesus. Pilate saw right through the religious leaders' thin ploy (Mark 15:10)—Jesus wasn't some dangerous revolutionary. He was a threat to the high council, but that didn't interfere with Roman interests. By all accounts, Jesus was completely innocent (Luke 23:13–15).

However, as Pilate made his determinations, the religious leaders stirred up the Jewish crowd, convincing them that Jesus was their enemy. Just a few days ago, Jesus had ridden into Jerusalem as a hero, the one the Jews hoped would deliver them from Roman rule (Luke 19:38).

The Pharisees turned that burning desire for freedom into hatred of Jesus. They claimed that Jesus was not their deliverer. He was a villainous fraud who committed blasphemy. By the time Pilate was ready to deliver his verdict, the confused crowd was frothing at the mouth. They wanted blood, and thanks to the religious leaders, Jesus was the target.

Pilate tried to reason with the hostile crowd, asking what fault they could find in Jesus. The Jewish leaders, clinging to any last desperate hope, threatened Pilate that by releasing Jesus, he'd be freeing an enemy of Caesar (John 19:12).

Fearful of a potential rebellion (Matthew 27:24), Pilate put the decision into the hands of the people. The custom of the time was that each year at Passover, the Romans would release one prisoner (John 18:39). Pilate gave the Jews a choice: Barabbas or Jesus?

This was a calculated move. Though the Jews didn't enjoy being under Roman rule, the religious leaders held a favorable position with the Romans, who didn't interfere much with their leadership. The Jewish leaders enjoyed wealth, power, and prominence among the Jews. Zealots such as Barabbas threatened to wreck the status quo and anger the Romans, upsetting the leaders' comfy position. Pilate figured that the Jewish leaders would feel more threatened by Barabbas and convince the people to let Jesus go.

He was shocked at how wrong he was.

Here lies the danger of just going along with the crowd. There wasn't a single individual among the people that Jesus had wronged. In fact, many of them had seen or heard of the miraculous works He had done that week in Jerusalem. Yet they not only chose to release Barabbas, but they also chanted at Pilate to crucify Jesus. A few influential voices turned a group of sound-minded individuals into a raving mob.

When tempted to make a decision simply because it's what everyone else is doing, keep Exodus 23:2 in mind: "You shall not fall in with the many to do evil, nor shall you bear witness in a lawsuit, siding with the many, so as to pervert justice."

Right now, picture the person you love more than any other; it could be a parent, friend, spouse, or personal hero. Mine would be my wife, Sarah. She's genuinely the kindest, sweetest, most thoughtful person I've ever met. She is my rock.

Now—and be warned, because this is going to be painful—picture your loved one on the cross. Really think about the details:

- The blood oozing from his or her forehead as a crown of thorns is forcefully applied.
- The cries of anguish as metal stakes are pounded into wrists and feet.
- The suffocation he or she experiences as lungs slowly give out.
- The desire for death mercifully to arrive, for that would be a release from this incredible suffering.

Just thinking about this scene brings tears to my eyes.

Now up the ante. A crowd had the chance to spare your beloved, but instead chose to free a terrorist.

That's essentially what happened here, only Jesus was the flawless, perfect Son of God, on earth solely to save the very people that clamored for Him to be nailed to a tree.

What's more, Barabbas was guilty of the very crime the Jews pinned on Jesus. When He was tried in front of the Jewish leaders, Jesus was accused of blasphemy, because He had declared Himself God (Matthew 26:62–66). But the Romans weren't concerned with Jewish religion and couldn't care less what Jesus called Himself. The Jewish leaders knew this, so when they presented their case to Pilate, they accused Jesus of leading a revolt against Rome (Luke 23:1–2)—which is exactly what Barabbas did.

We don't know what Barabbas did with his freedom. The Bible makes no mention of his future. Maybe he repented and lived an honest life. Perhaps he went back to his old lifestyle and was arrested again the next day. We have no idea.

All we know is he walked free, even as nails were hammered into Jesus' flesh. That center cross on which Jesus hung likely would have been Barabbas's destination had Jesus not taken his place.

And that is why you, my friend, are Barabbas.

You have sinned and failed to uphold God's Law. You are sentenced to an eternal death (Romans 6:23). You're a rebel just like Barabbas, and you deserve a painful end.

Fortunately, there is an Advocate to step into your place and take your suffering. Barabbas lucked out with a get-out-of-jail-free card. He did nothing to deserve this second chance. It was handed to him on a silver platter.

Look at Romans 8:1. "There is therefore now no condemnation for those who are in Christ Jesus." All humans are on death row, but Jesus granted us a reprieve. He took on our sin, our burden, all out of love (1 Peter 3:18).

When the crowds in Pilate's court shouted for Barabbas to be released and Jesus to be crucified, they were expressing the very thing Jesus was there to do.

Just think about that.

Barabbas was likely going to die from capital punishment that Friday. He had no future and no hope.

But Jesus stepped in and took Barabbas's place. The nails that belonged in Barabbas's hands and feet were hammered into those of Jesus. So what if He didn't deserve it? Jesus loved Barabbas, rebel that he was, enough to trade places with him.

And me.

And you.

No one is worthy of Christ's sacrifice, yet He gave it.

How does that make you feel about your forbidden tree?

You could return to your tree and eat the fruit as often as you like. Thanks to Jesus' death, you're not subject to God's judgment as Adam and Eve were. You could sin again and again and again, and still find redemption. You could rebel against your Creator.

But why would you?

Is that momentary pleasure really worth insulting your God, the One who created you and loves you so much that He won't destroy you despite your rebellion?

Look, I know it's not easy. Temptation is a massive struggle. But tough as it is, we must take 2 Timothy 2:22 to heart:

> So flee youthful passions and pursue righteousness, faith, love, and peace, along with those who call on the Lord from a pure heart.

Sadly, you will still rebel. That's the reality of our sinful nature.

But God loves rebels so much that He died for them.

Knowing that, however, doesn't mean that you should give up and indulge your sinful desires, knowing that God will always take you back. When you resist temptation and defy your rebellious nature, you honor God.

> Let us not grow weary of doing good, for in due season we will reap, if we do not give up. (Galatians 6:9)

Rebels can be cool. We can look up to them as role models. Who wouldn't want to be as suave as Han Solo, as brave as William Wallace, or as iron-willed as Katniss Everdeen? When you're passionate for a noble cause, you can accomplish great things and help people.

Just don't let your attitude invoke another movie title: *Rebel Without a Cause*. That's what fighting against God makes you.

CHAPTER 10

REVENGE

Do not repay evil for evil or reviling for reviling,
but on the contrary, bless, for to this you
were called, that you may obtain a blessing. (1 Peter 3:9)

The award-winning film *Gladiator* centers on a betrayed man's pursuit of revenge. When we first meet Maximus, he's an extremely successful general of the Roman legions. That is, until the new emperor, Commodus, betrays Maximus and murders his wife and son. Maximus is imprisoned and forced to fight as a gladiator for the enjoyment of the Roman masses.

Maximus is a skilled warrior, but it's his insatiable desire for revenge that drives him in each battle. He'll stop at nothing to kill anyone in his path and exact revenge on Commodus.

I still remember how the line about exacting vengeance was quoted in nearly every conversation among my friends in the months following the film's release. The line was so epic, the delivery so filled with passion and hatred, that it was inspiring—especially for a bunch of ten-year-old kids busy playing the video game *Super Smash Bros.*

Maximus is lionized for his bloodthirsty pursuit of revenge, and it's not hard to sympathize with his plight. His entire life was ripped away from him, and his last sight as a free man was of his slain family.

Plus, Commodus is the worst of the worst. He took the throne by suffocating his father. He fell in love with his sister. Threatened by Maximus's power and the respect he held within the nation, Commodus performed unspeakable, unthinkable acts to ensure Maximus wouldn't interrupt his plans. Commodus is a perfect villain—everyone in the audience is rooting against him. Even the most empathetic moviegoers can't find sympathy for this man.

On the flip side, who can't sympathize with Maximus? He is beloved because we can easily understand his motivation. Just imagine if someone arranged for the two people you love most to be killed; can't you feel your blood start to boil? The very idea is sickening and infuriating. I can feel my pulse quickening even writing these words.

So even as Maximus slays numerous enemies in the arena, stages a coup to overthrow Commodus, and eventually (I would say spoiler alert here, but the movie came out in 2000 and is a classic; if you haven't seen it at this point, that's on you) kills Commodus, we're rooting for him every step of the way. The amount of blood he sheds is of little importance; Maximus is our hero, and it's easy to justify his actions.

He had no choice but to fight for his family's memory. To take matters into his own hands.

Right?

Not quite. At least, not in God's eyes.

Much as we humans may glorify vengeance, God's not a big fan. The Bible is very clear on where God stands:

> You shall not take vengeance or bear a grudge against the sons of your own people, but you shall love your neighbor as yourself: I am the Lord. (Leviticus 19:18)

> Do not say, "I will repay evil"; wait for the Lord, and He will deliver you. (Proverbs 20:22)

> Let all bitterness and wrath and anger and clamor and slander be put away from you, along with all malice. Be kind to one another, tenderhearted, forgiving one another, as God in Christ forgave you. (Ephesians 4:31–32)

God not only frowns on revenge but also considers it evil. We're told hating our enemies, no matter what they have done, is wrong. Love is meant to be our default setting.

Most of us haven't experienced the type of emotional devastation Maximus felt in *Gladiator*, but I'm willing to bet you've experienced some level of betrayal in your life. Perhaps a co-worker went behind your back to take credit for your work or maybe even to get the promotion you deserved. Maybe your spouse was unfaithful. Perhaps you've been wrongly criticized by a family member.

Your desire to right your perceived wrongs might feel justified; trust me, no one holds a grudge like I do. But doing so is a meaningless exercise.

Just ask Jonah how his whole revenge strategy worked out.

Jonah

You didn't want to mess with Assyria in biblical times. The Assyrian empire was vast, powerful, and crawling with evil. It glorified heartless cruelty, and its capital, Nineveh, was known as "the bloody city, all full of lies and plunder" (Nahum 3:1). The people there were guilty of prostitution, idolatry, and evil plots against God. Their soldiers often razed the cities they conquered and tortured the defeated people. Opposing soldiers were burned, skinned alive, and had their tongues cut out, while women and children were taken captive as slaves.

Nineveh was the furnace that fueled the whole machine. Allow Nahum, one of Israel's prophets, to sum up the nature of the Ninevites:

> Woe to the bloody city, all full of lies and plunder—no end to the prey! The crack of the whip, and rumble of the wheel, galloping horse and bounding chariot! Horsemen charging, flashing sword and glittering spear, hosts of slain, heaps of corpses, dead bodies without end—they stumble over the bodies! And all for the countless whorings of the prostitute, graceful and of deadly charms, who betrays nations with her whorings, and peoples with her charms. (Nahum 3:1–4)

The Assyrians were the big kid on the playground who interrupts the younger kids' soccer game, pops their ball, and then gives them all atomic wedgies.

God gave Jonah the chance to punch the bully right in the face.

God instructed Jonah, an Israelite prophet around 750 BC, to deliver a damning message to the Ninevites:

> Arise, go to Nineveh, that great city, and call out against it, for their evil has come up before Me. (Jonah 1:2)

This is like telling an eight-year-old to go to the kitchen pantry and eat all the cookies they can find.

After years of seeing them kick his people around, Jonah despised the Ninevites. Now God was acknowledging they had gone too far, and the Ninevites would be destroyed for their cruelty.

Jonah would be the messenger to alert his enemies that doom was on the horizon, to rub the noses of his people's tormentors in the dirt. How do you beat that?

Only Jonah didn't want to do it.

In fact, the Bible doesn't even record a response from Jonah. All we know is he immediately tried to escape the Lord. He went to the nearest port and purchased a ticket to go to Tarshish, a land thousands of miles southwest of Israel.

Nineveh was a few hundred miles in the opposite direction.

The Bible says Jonah tried to run away from God (Jonah 1:2) because he had no interest in this mission. Growing up, I always assumed this was because Jonah was afraid of the Ninevites. Could you blame him? This was a rough crowd. Can you believe how they might treat an outsider, someone they would consider unfit for their presence, who arrived and declared judgment on them?

But the more times I read Jonah's story, the more I began to wonder if fear wasn't really his primary motivation in fleeing for Tarshish. Could it have been hate?

Jonah was afraid God would have mercy on the Ninevites. He was terrified by the very possibility that when presented with the news of their extinction, these people would repent, causing God to have mercy on them.

Jonah would rather see them be wiped from the face of the earth than have them be given a second chance.

Here's how Jonah saw it: in its current state, God planned on destroying the Ninevites. If Jonah visited and Nineveh repented, there was a small chance for redemption. But if he didn't visit them, then they would certainly be destroyed!

With that calculus in mind, Jonah fled for Tarshish. But he never made it.

You can't just reject God's plans like that. Like it or not, He has a way of redirecting your path to get you back where He wants your help—and God deeply desired that Jonah would deliver this critical message. He caused a great storm to rise up, one so powerful that it threatened to rip apart the ship Jonah was traveling in. Recognizing his sin and God's anger, Jonah revealed to the terrified sailors that he was the problem and they should toss him into the ocean. They reluctantly obliged, and the waves immediately calmed. As the sailors celebrated and offered sacrifices to God, a giant fish arrived and swallowed Jonah.

For three days, Jonah languished in the belly of the fish, left alone with only his thoughts, stomach fluids, and the partial corpses of smaller fish. Most illustrations of this journey depict Jonah seated comfortably in a cavernous space, just waiting for his fishy timeout to end. I imagine the reality was far worse: it was likely quite cramped, enough for most of us to experience extreme claustrophobia. Jonah was likely pelted with a wave of saltwater and fish guts every time his captor opened his mouth. And the smell—well, I don't need to go into detail there. Use your imagination.

Jonah cried out from "the belly of Sheol" (Jonah 2:2), a place of darkness where the dead go. He pleaded with the Lord, praying for deliverance, acknowledging God's goodness, and praising his Maker. Most importantly, look at the end of his prayer in Jonah 2:9:

> But I with the voice of thanksgiving will sacrifice to You; what I have vowed I will pay. Salvation belongs to the LORD!

These two sentences are all God wanted to hear from Jonah. First, Jonah promised he would deliver the message to the Ninevites, which was all God originally wanted. But we also see Jonah's change of heart. By refusing to go to Nineveh and denying his enemies a second chance, Jonah had taken salvation into his own hands. He had decided to play God.

God is the only one who can offer salvation (Acts 4:12; Matthew 19:25–26). As a prophet, Jonah knew this. But his hatred blinded him, and his suffering helped him find the right perspective.

With Jonah's moral compass now restored, God caused the fish to spit him back onto dry land. God repeated Jonah's mission to him, only now His directive had a strong undercurrent: "Get to Nineveh with My message—or else."

If being swallowed alive was the first round of punishment, Jonah didn't want to see what else God had in store. He hightailed it to Nineveh, where he shouted to the crowds: "Yet forty days, and Nineveh shall be overthrown!" (Jonah 3:4).

Translation: You've got forty days, and then you're all toast.

When I play this scene out in my mind, things get hostile quickly. First, the haughty Ninevites point and laugh at the insane peasant prophesying doom and gloom in the streets. As he persists, they become angry: "Who is this person? And who is he to tell us we'll be destroyed?" Then they gang up on Jonah and teach this unwelcome traveler a lesson.

But the Ninevites responded in surprising fashion. Rather than mob Jonah, they declared a fast and put on burlap clothing to express their remorse. The king of Nineveh traded his royal robes for burlap, sat on a heap of ashes, and sent a decree throughout the city that everyone must refrain from eating, turn from their evil ways, and pray earnestly to God. "Who knows?" he said. "God may turn and relent and turn from His fierce anger, so that we may not perish" (Jonah 3:9).

God was so moved by the Ninevites' change of heart that He reversed course and decided not to carry out the destruction He had promised.

God can get angry, but He's ultimately a God of mercy. He doesn't want to harm or destroy us. Rather, He brings us His Law and Gospel, providing yet another shot at redemption:

> If we confess our sins, He is faithful and just to forgive us our sins and to cleanse us from all unrighteousness. (1 John 1:9)

> Who is a God like You, pardoning iniquity and passing over transgression for the remnant of His inheritance? He does not retain His anger forever, because He delights in steadfast love. (Micah 7:18)

> The LORD is good to all, and His mercy is over all that He has made. (Psalm 145:9)

> The Lord is not slow to fulfill His promise as some count slowness, but is patient toward you, not wishing that any should perish, but that all should reach repentance. (2 Peter 3:9)

I could fill the next four pages with verses about God's mercy. On the other hand, He is also a just God who must, by His very being, adhere to the guidelines He set. He can only show forgiveness if He lays our guilt on Jesus and punishes Him in our place (which He accomplished on the cross). If we believe in and honor that sacrifice, show contrition, and honestly ask for forgiveness, He'll grant grace even to the worst of us.

This is exactly what Jonah feared.

His original nightmare had come to fruition. Rather than destroy the Ninevites, God had taken pity on them. These evil people would remain in power and loom over lesser nations, including Israel, like a dark cloud that threatened to unleash a devastating storm at any point. Jonah prayed to God in anger:

> O LORD, is not this what I said when I was yet in my country? That is why I made haste to flee to Tarshish; for I knew that You are a gracious God and merciful, slow to anger and abounding in steadfast love, and relenting from disaster. Therefore now, O LORD, please take my life from me, for it is better for me to die than to live. (Jonah 4:2–3)

Jonah knew God possessed this incredible level of mercy. He was so distressed by this turn of events that he requested death over living in a world where Nineveh would continue to exist.

I can sympathize with Jonah to some extent. He was hoping God would vanquish the Ninevites, freeing his people from ever experiencing their torment again. Nineveh well deserved what it had coming. For God to perform an about-face in Israel's moment of vengeance was incredibly disappointing.

But time and time again, the Bible tells us retaliation isn't the right response. It might feel great in the moment, but that pleasure is fleeting. Rather, futile as it may seem, we should treat our enemies with kindness:

> Do not repay evil for evil or reviling for reviling, but on the contrary, bless, for to this you were called, that you may obtain a blessing. (1 Peter 3:9)

> See that no one repays anyone evil for evil, but always seek to do good to one another and to everyone. (1 Thessalonians 5:15)

> But I say to you who hear, Love your enemies, do good to those who hate you, bless those who curse you, pray for those who abuse you. (Luke 6:27–28)

That doesn't sound as satisfying, does it?

Actually, repaying evil with good not only pleases God, but it also hurts your enemy more than you know: "If your enemy is hungry, give him bread to eat, and if he is thirsty, give him water to drink, for you will heap burning coals on his head, and the Lord will reward you" (Proverbs 25:21–22).

Let's use an overbearing boss as an example. This boss belittles you, routinely expects you to stay after hours, and never seems to have the time of day to answer your questions. It would be pretty easy to dislike this person, right? Subconsciously, you think bad thoughts about him every time you see him. You gossip and complain about him to your co-workers, who feel the same way.

But what if this boss came up to you one day and offered to take you out to lunch, his treat, wherever you want to go? As you wait for your meal, he apologizes to you for his actions and promises to treat you better moving forward. Then he starts asking about your life and tries to get to know you better as a person, showing you the respect you have desired for years.

Such a change of heart would be both surprising and indicting. Maybe your boss deserved the things you thought and said about him, but then his kindness makes you feel confusion and guilt. Suddenly, he has turned the tables on you; *you* feel like the bad guy, not him.

Now flip that scenario around with your enemies. When you genuinely love them, forgive them, and treat them well, they feel ashamed for what they have said and done to you. Hopefully, your love and kindness will stir a heart of repentance in them. And the Lord will reward you.

Win-win.

But wait; someone does evil and just gets away scot-free? When misbehavior actually earns a person kindness, it seems like an odd way to administer justice.

Don't worry, justice is coming; it's just not coming from you.

> This is evidence of the righteous judgment of God, that you may be considered worthy of the kingdom of God, for which you are also suffering—since indeed God considers it just to repay with affliction those who afflict you, and to grant relief to you who are afflicted as well as to us, when the Lord Jesus is revealed from heaven with His mighty angels in flaming fire, inflicting vengeance on those who do not know God and on those who do not obey the gospel of our Lord Jesus. (2 Thessalonians 1:5–8)

> Vengeance is Mine, and recompense, for the time when their foot shall slip; for the day of their

> calamity is at hand, and their doom comes swiftly. (Deuteronomy 32:35)
>
> For we know Him who said, "Vengeance is Mine; I will repay." And again, "The Lord will judge His people." (Hebrews 10:30)

Let God take care of the vengeance. He understands who deserves punishment and who doesn't, far more than you do. When the time is right, He'll make sure those who do wrong get what's coming to them.

Consider the Ninevites. Though they originally responded positively to Jonah's message, the good times didn't last. Check out the book of Nahum, which was penned about one hundred years after Jonah's ministry. Nahum declared that the Assyrians "will be cut down and pass away" (Nahum 1:12) and would be devoured by locusts (Nahum 3:15). In fact, the entire Book of Nahum is essentially a warning of reckoning for the evil nation.

If only Jonah had known all this was coming when he wished for death some time before.

Jonah shouldn't have needed proof to know that God was just. There was plenty of biblical evidence. But he didn't want to wait for Nineveh to receive its comeuppance. He wanted instant gratification; that's why he had tried to take matters into his own hands.

Stephen

On the flip side of the coin is Stephen, a critical member of the Early Church after Jesus' resurrection. Like Jonah, he was called to bring an unpopular message to a powerful group. But instead of running away, Stephen charged headfirst into the hornet's nest, forsaking all personal safety for God's mission.

This decision ended in a brutal death that prevented him from seeing the long-term effects of Christ's Church. But given that Stephen's actions set many important gears in motion for what was to come, I'm willing to bet he wouldn't change a thing.

The religious leaders thought that by killing Jesus, they would silence His message and crush any potential impact He might have had. They didn't understand that Jesus' death, resurrection, and ascension allowed the Holy Spirit to enter the believers (John 16:12–14), making them bolder and more powerful than before (Acts 2:1–41). These believers formed a community in which they shared everything they had, selling all property and possessions to help those in need (Acts 2:42–47). Never in human history has there been a better physical representation of the selfless love of the Trinity. These people lived and worked together for one purpose: to glorify God and spread His message.

Jesus' apostles, especially Peter and John, were on fire, healing the sick and those possessed by evil spirits, escaping prison, and putting the religious leaders to shame with their biblical knowledge. But they quickly realized they needed help to run this new community, and they appointed seven men to organize the daily distribution of food among the believers.

Though these were all great men, Stephen stood out above the rest. Of the seven, Acts 6:5 singles out Stephen as "a man full of faith and of the Holy Spirit." Then in Acts 6:8, we see Stephen performing miracles and signs among the people, "full of grace and power."

So impactful was his presence that the synagogue of the Freedmen felt threatened by his teachings. Their influence slipping away, they persuaded some men to lie about Stephen, saying he was blaspheming Moses and God. The elders and teachers of religious law, happy for any excuse to silence one of Jesus' followers, had Stephen arrested and brought before the high council.

This was Stephen's Jonah moment. He could have chosen to board the boat for Tarshish and deny everything; doing so would have likely earned him his freedom back.

But Stephen tightened his bootstraps and marched for Nineveh, with no regard for his personal safety. When questioned, Stephen's face became "like the face of an angel" (Acts 6:15). He was full of the Spirit.

Game on.

Given the opportunity to deny the false accusations, Stephen launched into a historical diatribe that concluded with a brutal takedown of the religious leaders:

> You stiff-necked people, uncircumcised in heart and ears, you always resist the Holy Spirit. As your fathers did, so do you. Which of the prophets did your fathers not persecute? And they killed those who announced beforehand the coming of the Righteous One, whom you have now betrayed and murdered, you who received the law as delivered by angels and did not keep it. (Acts 7:51–53)

Stephen had to know as he was speaking these words that they might be his last. Rarely did people talk to the religious leaders like this and come out all right on the other side. This was the same high council that a few months earlier had condemned Jesus to death before handing Him over to Pontius Pilate. He was signing his own death warrant.

As the Jewish leaders became enraged, Stephen doubled down: "Full of the Holy Spirit, [he] gazed into heaven and saw the glory of God, and Jesus standing at the right hand of God. And he said, "Behold, I see the heavens opened, and the Son of Man standing at the right hand of God" (Acts 7:55–56).

That was just too much for Stephen's accusers. They dragged him into the street, formed a circle around him, and hurled large stones at him until he died. Think how many cuts, wounds, and broken bones Stephen endured before one of the heavy rocks mercifully struck his head and turned the lights out forever.

And yet, look at Stephen's final act: "And as they were stoning Stephen, he called out, 'Lord Jesus, receive my spirit.' And falling to his knees he cried out with a loud voice, 'Lord, do not hold this sin against them.' And when he had said this, he fell asleep" (Acts 7:59–60).

"Do not hold this sin against them."

Wow.

When was the last time you thought that about your enemy? The person who gossips about you at work? The parent who was too hard on you growing up? The unfaithful spouse who left you?

Was your first thought to pray for their soul?

I know that's not my first response.

Quite the opposite, I'm afraid to say.

And yet Stephen saved his last breath to plead for the very men who were launching rocks at his head. As his bones cracked and his life faded, he asked God to have mercy on his accusers.

It brings to mind some of Jesus' final words on the cross: "Father, forgive them, for they know not what they do" (Luke 23:34).

And with that, Stephen became the first Christian martyr.

Compared to other biblical characters, Stephen's story is brief. But in just two chapters, Stephen sets some incredible acts in motion. As a result of the persecution against Christians that Stephen's stoning introduced, believers were scattered all over the region. These believers traveled as far as Phoenicia, Cyprus, and Antioch of Syria (Acts 11:19), where they introduced new believers to the faith.

But the most impactful part of Stephen's ministry was Saul.

Saul, also known as Paul, is one of the most important characters in biblical history; one could argue that no one outside of Jesus Himself made a greater impact for the Kingdom. He started numerous churches and became one of the most important spiritual advocates who shared Christ's message with the Gentiles. Our world would look completely different today without Saul's work.

But Saul didn't start on a noble path. When we first meet Saul, he's on the opposite side. A devout Jew and zealous Pharisee who had undergone intense religious training, Saul was offended by this new movement and wanted to squash it. He was present at Stephen's stoning and nodded in approval as stones broke Stephen's body.

The Bible tells us that "there arose on that day a great persecution against the church in Jerusalem, and they were all scattered throughout the regions of Judea and Samaria, except the apostles" (Acts 8:1). Saul led the charge most furiously, traveling far and wide to drag Christians out of their homes and toss them into prison. It was on one of these hunting missions that he was temporarily blinded and visited by Jesus, whose words led to Paul's conversion.

While I encourage you to read that story in Acts 9, I want to focus on Stephen's impact here. Why was it "on that day" that this wave of persecution arose? Several Christians, including Peter and John, had publicly spoken out against the religious leaders. The Christians had performed miracles, and their newly-formed community had surely caught the attention of the Pharisees.

So what was it about this day that made them feel the Christians were a real threat?

I think it was those final words Stephen spoke.

"Do not hold this sin against them."

Capital punishment was a part of Jewish law, though at this point, Rome had suspended the council's right to administer it. That's why Jesus was brought before and tried by Pilate. But the Jewish leaders were so enraged, they took matters into their own hands and committed the equivalent of an illegal lynching. This was a truly hateful, heinous, defiant act.

When Stephen declined to plead for his life or curse them, but instead reached out to God on their behalf, it was quite the shock.

Imagine the shiver that must have run down Paul's spine when he heard those words. I think it was that moment that he realized this wasn't some run-of-the-mill revolution. The Jews had plenty of experience squashing new religions or minor riots.

But this was something different. Here was a man who not only was willing to die for his faith but who also cared more about the well-being of those killing him than about himself.

I think it was in that moment that Saul realized Christianity was something real, and this movement threatened everything he knew about religion.

When you pray for those who persecute you, you don't have to worry about sparking a wave of persecution (at least, I hope not). But your actions and prayers may cause others to take an extra second to think, "What is it with this person? What would drive them to pray for me?"

"What do they have in their life that I don't?"

Thus, they're exposed to this new concept of faith.

That in itself is such a blessing! You can make an eternal impact on someone's life by foregoing revenge and showing them a new way: Jesus. And God promises additional blessings when you turn vengeance over to Him.

Of course, there's no better example of this than Jesus Himself. If anyone deserved to take revenge, it was the man who was publicly ridiculed, shamed, and executed for no reason. But He took it all for you.

Let's examine just a short portion of His suffering. In John 18, Jesus was arrested and questioned by Roman governor Pontius Pilate. Though Pilate could find no fault with Jesus, the Jewish crowd demanded that He be executed and that known criminal Barabbas be freed (John 18:38–40).

In an attempt to pacify the bloodthirsty crowd, Pilate had Jesus flogged. I think it's critically important that we understand how excruciatingly painful flogging is. The prisoner was stripped and had his hands tied to a post above his head. Then two soldiers took turns lashing him with leather whips tipped with chips of bone or lead. The sharp tips tore the victim's shoulders and back to ribbons. Some authors refer to flagellation as half-death, as the wounded often perished soon after.

That was only the beginning. Think of the last time you touched a thorn on a tree or rose bush. It stung, right? And you probably didn't touch it hard enough to draw blood.

Well, Jesus had a crown woven of those same thorns forced

down upon His head. The scalp is one of the most vascular areas of the body, so this likely caused copious amounts of bleeding.

Then the Roman soldiers threw a purple robe around Jesus' shoulders to mock Him, saying, "Hail, King of the Jews" (John 19:3). Purple is the color associated with royalty, though these men clearly weren't honoring Jesus. As He bled profusely and clung to life, they made fun of Him and struck Him on the head with a stick.

Jesus was tortured and humiliated by the very people He had once created—the same people He had come to save.

At any point, Jesus could have taken revenge. He could have said, "Wait, I'm sacrificing Myself for these fallen people, and this is how they treat Me? Forget this." He could have rained down fire on His torturers or gone Hulk-mode to escape them. He could have just snapped His fingers and rendered them all useless.

But He didn't.

He took their scorn and absorbed the shame. He felt each blow, each tearing of His skin. He accepted the thorns as they pierced His forehead.

All because He loved you, and this needed to happen in order to save you.

In fact, He not only allowed these terrible things to happen to Him, but He also called out on behalf of His persecutors. As He hung on the cross, He used the little breath left in His lungs to plead with God, "Father, forgive them, for they know not what they do" (Luke 23:34).

With Jesus as an example, what right do you have to take revenge?

The One who took on more pain than you can imagine, despite the knowledge that you would routinely betray and fail Him, didn't take revenge. He chose the most humbling route possible, all because He wanted the best possible future for you.

> He was oppressed, and He was afflicted, yet He opened not His mouth; like a lamb that is led to the slaughter, and like a sheep that before its shearers is silent, so He opened not His mouth. (Isaiah 53:7)

Maximus's thirst for revenge may be epic, but it's not applicable in reality. But with God's promise of blessings in mind, we are reminded that no matter how difficult it may be, forgiveness, not revenge, is the right path.

CHAPTER 11

Short-Term Thinking

Precious treasure and oil are in a wise man's dwelling, but a foolish man devours it. (Proverbs 21:20)

Here's a fun exercise: think of the Bible in terms of the high-school social structure.

David is the prom king, the superstar athlete, and the one who always has the prettiest date for homecoming.

Paul is the no-nonsense intellect who isn't afraid to debate a teacher if he disagrees.

Martha is the straight-A student who spends all her time either studying or volunteering.

And Esau is the meathead football player who can always be found in either the weight room or the cafeteria. He possesses tremendous physical strength but isn't exactly the sharpest tool in the shed. If you play your cards right, he'll trade his college football scholarship for your brownie at lunchtime.

Esau

As a young man, Esau had a way of prioritizing what was happening in the next fifteen minutes, not the next fifteen days (much less years). He lived in the moment and paid little attention to the future. If the responsible investor puts his money into savings accounts and retirement funds, Esau is the man living paycheck to paycheck with a small shoebox of money underneath his bed.

His failure to examine the long-term consequences of his actions ended up altering his life.

Let's jump back all the way to Genesis 25, when twins Esau and Jacob were born as Isaac's offspring. Because Esau was born first, he was technically the elder son, a distinction that earned him Isaac's birthright and blessing. To get the context of the situation, it's important to understand how critical those terms were in biblical times.

- The birthright granted the oldest son not only a double portion of the family inheritance but also the honor of becoming the family leader when his father passed.
- The blessing may not have been as valuable in monetary terms, but it was extremely important and carried great spiritual benefits (Genesis 27:28–29).

By the sheer luck of being born first, Esau inherited some significant advantages over his little brother.

But as they grew, it became clear that even if Isaac were to choose who received these gifts, it would be Esau. Esau was a skilled hunter and outdoorsman, the kind of person that would make Bear Grylls look like a glamper. He brought home delicious wild game, which won his father's affection (I can appreciate a man who thinks with his stomach first).

Then there was Jacob, a mild-mannered mama's boy who stuck around the house and was favored by Rebekah, Isaac's wife.

But for all the physical, manly advantages Esau may have had over his younger brother, Jacob ran laps around him when it came to intelligence. Jacob was a smart, cunning strategist, while Esau—well, he wasn't exactly nuclear-physicist material.

One day, Esau returned particularly exhausted from a hunt (Genesis 25:27–34). Jacob was making a stew, and the famished Esau asked for a bowl. Jacob demanded Esau's birthright in return, and Esau, in his brilliance, decided that a bowl of stew was more important than his future. "I am about to die," Esau said. "Of what use is a birthright to me?" (Genesis 25:32).

Maybe Esau would have starred on the high school drama team too.

Oh, and that better have been the best bowl of soup the world has ever seen.

Esau thought with his stomach instead of his brain, casually tossing away important benefits he wouldn't be able to get back. There was no return policy on this bowl of soup.

By giving up these rights, he showed a complete disregard for the spiritual blessings that lay in his future.

While it's possible that Esau was truly about to die of starvation, he was probably just being dramatic. Genesis 25:34 says that "Esau despised his birthright"; the honor doesn't appear to have meant much to him.

Esau allowed the pressure of the moment to warp his perspective. He was clearly very hungry and felt food was his primary objective. It's easy to look at his actions and think, "What a dummy," but are we not guilty of the same thing?

It's actually quite common to value short-term gain over long-term rewards. In our microwave society, we're constantly thinking about what would make us happiest right now.

Think about the couple that engages in sex before marriage, valuing the momentary pleasure over their sexual purity. Or the college student that cheats on an exam, staining his integrity. Or the employee who gossips against a co-worker, choosing the fleeting benefit of human acceptance over God's commands.

Every time we engage in sin, we're telling God the short-lived pleasure that comes from our disobedience is worth more than our place in heaven. We trade our birthright for a proverbial bowl of stew—something worth far less than our spiritual future.

Jesus' sacrifice erased that consequence and assured us an eternity in heaven if we repent (Ephesians 1:7–8), but the fact of the matter still stands—each sin is a ticket to hell (Romans 5:12). While we have the knowledge that Christ's death brought us life, we also know that the hammer that pounded the nails into His flesh was forged from our wrongdoings. Our sins, not the Roman soldiers or the Jewish leaders, were what ultimately put Him on that cross.

Speaking of Jesus, no one understood the long game better than He did.

Just look at His agony in Matthew 26 when Jesus and His disciples arrived at the Garden of Gethsemane to pray. By the following afternoon, Jesus would be arrested, beaten, humiliated, whipped, insulted, mutilated, condemned, belittled, and ultimately killed.

He knew all of this. He could see it just as clearly as you're seeing the words on this page right now.

It tore Him up inside. His "soul [was] very sorrowful, even to death" (Matthew 26:38). He separated Himself from the disciples to pray one-on-one with His Father, at which point Jesus became so distressed that "His sweat became like great drops of blood falling down to the ground" (Luke 22:44). This condition is called *hematohidrosis*, and it occurs when a person is under such extreme physical or emotional stress that the capillary blood vessels that feed the sweat glands burst, which causes the sweat glands to produce blood.

Jesus' future was so terrifying and stressful that He was looking for an alternative path.

From the first time Adam and Eve sinned, a wall was erected between fallen humans and our perfect God. Our sin earned us a place in hell. The only way to satisfy that transaction was for someone to die in our place.

That person had to be Jesus. It would be extremely painful from a physical, emotional, and spiritual standpoint, but if Jesus could endure it, then the barrier between God and humanity would be torn down. The Holy Spirit could become our Advocate (John 14:26), and we would have full access to God.

That long-term goal was Jesus' ultimate goal. There's nothing He wants more than to be more connected to you.

But the short-term path to reach that goal was more brutal than any human had and ever will have to face.

So Jesus cried out to God. He begged His Father, "Let this cup pass from Me" (Matthew 26:39). Was there any other way to accomplish the mission?

But even as Jesus made His request, He knew the answer. This was the only way.

So Jesus bit the bullet.

Long-term goals beat out short-term suffering.

"Nevertheless, not as I will, but as You will," He prayed (Matthew 26:39). And again a short time later, "My Father, if this cannot pass unless I drink it, Your will be done" (Matthew 26:42).

Jesus gets it. He's been there. He understands the strong pull of short-term pleasures and relief.

Yet He resisted and endured, and now your soul is connected to His. The payoff was worth it.

Jesus also understands that as flawed, sinful humans, we're not always going to make the right choice. We're going to prioritize our immediate future over our eternal life. We're going to choose sin over Him.

We'll trade our birthright for soup.

That doesn't mean He'll snatch away your salvation. He still loves you (Romans 8:38–39).

But we should still aim to be better. We must respond to God's love, learn from our mistakes, and strive to prioritize the long view. That's what Esau did.

Things got even worse for our shortsighted friend. Recall how the firstborn son received both his father's birthright and his blessing? Esau stupidly bartered away the former, but at least he still had Isaac's blessing.

That is, until Jacob and his mother, Rebekah, tricked Isaac—who at this point was very old and nearly blind—into giving his blessing to the wrong son (Genesis 27). When Isaac and Esau discovered the treachery, there was nothing they could do. The blessing was binding.

Can't you just hear the heartbreak in Isaac's voice in Genesis 27:37? "Behold, I have made [Jacob] lord over you, and all his brothers I have given to him for servants, and with grain and wine I have sustained him. What then can I do for you, my son?"

Gut-wrenching stuff. Through the pages, you can almost feel Esau's extreme sorrow transform into bitter rage. It was time for his brother to pay.

His fiery anger burned so hot that he plotted to kill his brother. Jacob grew wise to this plan, escaped to Paddan-aram, got married (twice), had enough kids to field a baseball team, got rich, and underwent a lot of maturation. Then God instructed him to return home, where angry brother Esau lay in wait.

We don't know what happened in Esau's life between Jacob's departure and his return. At least twenty years passed, and it appears our brothers had no contact. As Jacob approached his homeland, he was so fearful for the safety of his family that he sent ahead lavish gifts to his brother (Genesis 32:13–16) and divided his family into two different groups, hoping one could escape if Esau's men attacked. When he came face-to-face with Esau, he bowed seven times before him, a sign of respect typically reserved for kings.

Put yourself in Esau's shoes. The man who stole your life from you is now groveling at your feet. He's surrounded by your loyal men who will, without question, execute your command.

What would you do?

Esau did the unthinkable and threw a big bear hug around his brother, welcoming him home.

Esau may not have been a scholar, but God showed him a valuable lesson during Jacob's absence. It was better to bury the hatchet and forgive his brother rather than carry a grudge. He allowed peace to overcome the anger that consumed him as a youth.

Here lies the true beauty of Esau's growth. Rather than enjoy the short-term satisfaction of revenge, he valued a long-term relationship with his brother.

Esau didn't know it, but he was putting into action a future command from Jesus, laid out in Matthew 5:38–39: "You have heard that it was said, 'An eye for an eye and a tooth for a tooth.' But I say to you, Do not resist the one who is evil. But if anyone slaps you on the right cheek, turn to him the other also."

What Jacob did was sneaky, false, and wrong. But Jesus calls us not only to forgive those who wrong us but also to bless them: "But I say to you, Love your enemies and pray for those who persecute you, so that you may be sons of your Father who is in heaven. For He makes His sun rise on the evil and on the good, and sends rain on the just and on the unjust" (Matthew 5:44–45).

That's exactly what Esau did. He turned down Jacob's gift, insisting Jacob didn't need to buy back his love, and provided men to protect Jacob on his journey home.

I don't think Esau gets enough credit for his maturity and transformation in the discussion of biblical heroes. The stereotype of the dumb jock suggests they live in high school forever, always wearing the letter jacket, talking about the glory days, and exaggerating their statistics.

But sometimes the jock grows and becomes a great man who makes a real difference.

Taking the long view is not an easy lesson to master. It often takes a lifetime to grasp, and most don't even get it by then! Even Paul, one of the greatest heroes in the Bible, needed some serious lessons in humility before he understood that his spirituality was more important than his momentary desires.

But boy, when he got it, Paul was all in.

Paul

We took a look at Saul's conversion back on page 11. To recap,

Saul was a zealous Jew, a hunter of Christians, eager to stomp out the embers of Jesus' movement.

Then he got a heavenly wake-up call (Acts 9:1–19) and changed his tune completely. He went from one of Satan's top weapons to a devout Christ-follower in the matter of a few days.

To say Paul was wholly bought-in is an understatement.

That vigor made Paul an incredible asset for the young Church. While we don't have the official statistics, I feel relatively safe in saying that no one (except maybe Peter or John) showed more people Jesus' love and led them to faith.

This fact was not lost on his former employers. The Jewish leaders did everything they could to silence Paul. Paul was threatened (Acts 22:22), beaten (Acts 21:30–31; 2 Corinthians 11:23), arrested (Acts 16:23–24; 21:33), ridiculed (Acts 26:24), whipped (2 Corinthians 11:24), stoned (2 Corinthians 11:25), and wrongly accused (Acts 25:7).

The Jews conspired to kill him (Acts 23:12–13), and they eventually succeeded—an outcome Paul knew was coming (2 Timothy 4:6–8). Paul spent about five years of his life in custody before he was executed under orders of the Roman governor.

Our man certainly went through the ringer.

And yet, Paul took it all on the chin like a champ. At no point did he seem to slow down or become dissuaded from his mission. The Jews' attempts to silence him only seemed to turn up his volume as he relentlessly worked to spread the Good News.

Paul went on three massive missionary journeys and started more than ten churches along the way. He played an immeasurably impactful role in showing the Gentiles that they were not only accepted by God (Acts 13:47) but also loved more than they could even understand, opening millions of people to Jesus' teachings.

His short-term future was constantly marked by suffering: arrests, mockery, lashings, and chains. But the long-term future was more souls saved for heaven, and that was Paul's top priority.

The closest we see him come to giving in comes in Philippians. Paul wrote this letter to the believers in Philippi while imprisoned in Rome. He had planted a church in Philippi during his second missionary journey and had developed a special love for the people there (Philippians 1:7–8).

Paul wrote the Philippians to explain the joy that comes not only from serving and believing but also from suffering for God. For a moment, he allowed himself to think what it would be like to be free of his life's tribulations:

> For to me to live is Christ, and to die is gain. If I am to live in the flesh, that means fruitful labor for me. Yet which I shall choose I cannot tell. I am hard pressed between the two. My desire is to depart and be with Christ, for that is far better. (Philippians 1:21–23)

Paul was ready to die.

To be clear, Paul wasn't considering suicide. But when he looked at his life, he saw two doors:

- **Door A:** Remain on earth, where he was consistently ridiculed, hunted, imprisoned, and physically harmed.
- **Door B:** Die and go to heaven, where he would get to meet his Lord and Savior, worshiping Him free of pain or fear for his safety.

Which option sounds better?

Paul just wanted to be with God. He was always telling others of the wonders of heaven and the exciting future of physically being with Jesus. He was anxious to experience those things himself.

In the short term, death was actually a great option. Goodbye, prison. Goodbye, suffering. Hello, heaven.

But unlike Esau, Paul was a long-term thinker.

> But to remain in the flesh is more necessary on your account. Convinced of this, I know that I will remain and continue with you all, for your progress and joy in the faith, so that in me you may have ample cause to glory in Christ Jesus, because of my coming to you again. (Philippians 1:24–26)

The young believers and churches he had planted still needed him. If Paul left, it would be like a lioness abandoning her cubs on the African plain, exposing the youngsters to predators. Their chances of survival significantly decrease without her.

Imagine if Mr. Miyagi left Daniel LaRusso after one training session (*The Karate Kid*), or if Yoda gave up on Luke Skywalker early in his Jedi training (*Star Wars*). The heroes of these movies had great potential, but they needed someone wiser and more experienced to show them the ropes before they were ready to fight on their own.

And so Paul remained.

The long-term livelihood of the Church was more important than his short-term well-being. His time in heaven would come. But now? Now he was needed on earth.

Paul's attitude makes me think of Rocky Balboa in the famous boxing movie *Rocky*. A scrappy nobody from Philadelphia, Rocky is a decided underdog in a match against world champion Apollo Creed.

And Apollo beats the snot out of him.

Rocky's face and body are peppered with powerful punches from his opponent. He gets knocked down and is so woozy he can barely get to his feet again. His nose is broken by one of Apollo's hooks. By the end of the fight, Rocky's eyes are nearly swollen shut from abuse, and he's so tired he can barely lift his gloves to deflect Apollo's jabs.

Yet right before the final round, he turns to his trainer and, between exhausted breaths, mutters to his trainer not to stop the fight, or else.

It would have been so much easier for Rocky to throw in the towel. He had proven his point. Rocky wasn't expected to last more than a few rounds against Apollo; the mere fact that he was still in the fight was an inspiration to millions.

But that wasn't enough. The mission wasn't complete, and Rocky wouldn't stop until he saw the end, no matter how much punishment he had to undergo.

Unlike Rocky, Paul was fighting for something larger than himself. He was fighting for Jesus, the One who had shown him so much love and compassion. Given how much Jesus had given up for him, stopping wasn't an option in Paul's eyes.

Like Jesus in the Garden of Gethsemane, Paul saw an easier path, one that involved far less suffering on his part. It was no doubt appealing, but he didn't allow his mind to entertain the thought. God hadn't called him to heaven yet, and until He did, Paul was going to fight his hardest to help more people come to Jesus.

"And let us not grow weary of doing good, for in due season

we will reap, if we do not give up," Paul wrote in his Letter to the Galatians (6:9).

Earlier, in a letter to believers in Rome, he wrote:

> Through Him we have also obtained access by faith into this grace in which we stand, and we rejoice in hope of the glory of God. Not only that, but we rejoice in our sufferings, knowing that suffering produces endurance, and endurance produces character, and character produces hope, and hope does not put us to shame, because God's love has been poured into our hearts through the Holy Spirit who has been given to us. (Romans 5:2–5)

I'm not going to lie and say that making this life change is easy. Prioritizing one's long-term well-being is often more difficult than focusing on short-term gains. What sounds better: eating a piece of double-layer chocolate cake or going for a five-mile run? One is going to taste really delicious in the moment, while the other is going to bring about fatigue and discomfort.

But the joy from the cake is fleeting, and consistently partaking in such sweets is harmful to one's long-term health. On the other hand, that run makes your body stronger and may very well help you live a longer, healthier life.

Esau took the chocolate cake.

Paul went for the run.

And Jesus *definitely* ran an ultramarathon.

Put down the fork and reach for your running shoes. You'll be better in the long run.

CHAPTER 12

VANITY

Humble yourselves, therefore, under the mighty hand of God so that at the proper time He may exalt you. (1 Peter 5:6)

Imagine being Larry Jordan.

Is that name not ringing any bells? Let's try again.

Imagine being Larry Jordan, older brother of Michael Jordan, the greatest basketball player of all time.

Michael was an international superstar. When he walked into a room, every head turned. Simply slapping his logo onto a pair of sneakers doubled their price.

Now put yourself in Larry's shoes every time he met someone and his brother's identity was discovered. The new acquaintance would be so excited, they couldn't contain themselves:

- "You're his brother? Michael was my favorite player!"
- "I was there when he scored forty-four points against the Knicks in the playoffs. What a game!"
- "What's he like in person?"
- "Do you think you could get me an autograph?"

Larry's life was likely Michael, Michael, Michael, nonstop. People saw him as Michael Jordan's brother, not Larry Jordan.

I don't know about you, but that would drive me up a wall.

To top it off, Larry Jordan was a very good basketball player in his own right. Eleven months Michael's senior, Larry also played at the University of North Carolina. Michael credits Larry and their athletic competitions for helping him develop the infamous competitive streak that defined his career.

Clifton "Pop" Herring, the brothers' basketball coach at Emsley A. Laney High School, even believes Larry could have been a better player than Michael.

Larry Jordan was no slouch when it came to basketball. But he wasn't Michael.

Few humans can understand that intense pressure put on them by a younger sibling's success, and the overwhelming feeling of being overshadowed.

I'm willing to bet Aaron could relate.

Aaron

Aaron was Moses' older brother, but he spent most of his life taking the backseat to him. For instance, when I mentioned to my wife that I was writing about Aaron for this chapter, she responded, "Who?" Upon being reminded that Moses had a brother, she replied, "Oh, yeah, that guy!"

That guy.

When God called on Moses to lead the Israelites out of Egyptian bondage (Exodus 3:1–4:17), Aaron wasn't even a part of the initial plans. Moses, terrified of returning to Egypt (which he had escaped after murdering an Egyptian slave driver), blubbered that he was "slow of speech and tongue" (Exodus 3:10). (By the way, considering this man was one of the greatest leaders in human history, I'm not buying it.) Only then did God relent and allow Aaron to tag along.

> Then the anger of the Lord was kindled against Moses and He said, "Is there not Aaron, your brother, the Levite? I know that he can speak well. Behold, he is coming out to meet you, and when he sees you, he will be glad in his heart. You shall speak to him and put the words in his mouth, and I will be with your mouth and with his mouth and will teach you both what to do. He shall speak for you to the people, and he shall be your mouth, and you shall be as God to him." (Exodus 4:14–16)

Put the words in his mouth.

He shall be your mouth.

You shall be as God to him.

God might as well have stamped the words "Second Fiddle" on Aaron's forehead; that's how obviously he was the sidekick.

To his credit, Aaron carried out most of his mission as a loyal companion without a single complaint. He readily accepted his role from the get-go and had his brother's back every step of the way. The words God gave him to speak put him in an instrumental role in convincing Pharaoh to let the Israelites go.

But as the journey across the desert to the Promised Land wore on, Moses' higher standing began to eat at Aaron. Moses bossed his brother around (Exodus 16:33). He got to conduct miracles, such as using his staff to bring water out of a rock and soothe the parched masses (Exodus 17:1–6). Moses alone was allowed to meet with God face-to-face on Mount Sinai (Exodus 19) to receive the Ten Commandments.

By that point (about two months after the Israelites departed Egypt), Aaron was sick of being number 2. When the opportunity to play hero arose, he jumped at it.

God had quite a lot of instructions to give to Moses (the second half of Exodus and all of Leviticus), and their meeting on Mount Sinai lasted forty days. The Israelites, who had by then built up a solid reputation as a whiny, cantankerous lot (more on that in a minute), came to complain to Aaron. Where was Moses, their fearless leader? And what of this God he claimed would lead them to this mythical "land flowing with milk and honey" (Exodus 3:8)?

Keep in mind, these are the same people who, just months prior, were brutally overworked slaves. Not only had God freed them, but He had also provided food, water, and victory over their enemies (Exodus 17:8–13).

Dory, the memory-challenged fish from *Finding Nemo*, had better recall.

Frustrated, the people gathered and came to Aaron:

> Up, make us gods who shall go before us. As for this Moses, the man who brought us up out of the land of Egypt, we do not know what has become of him. (Exodus 32:1)

Let's just pause briefly and admire the sheer lunacy of that statement. What's the point of worshiping a god you know is fabricated? If you're doubting the God you've witnessed perform actual miracles, what on earth makes you think some human-created idol is going to make everything better?

Aaron was a smart man. He no doubt saw the stupidity in this ridiculous request. Maybe Moses and God's retreat was taking longer than expected, but Aaron knew they were coming back. He also knew erecting a false god was not only pointless but also a slap in the face to his all-powerful Maker.

This was a very bad idea.

And yet look at his response: "Take off the rings of gold that are in the ears of your wives, your sons, and your daughters, and bring them to me" (Exodus 32:2). He melted this gold down and constructed a calf, built an altar to it, and said, "Tomorrow shall be a feast to the Lord" (Exodus 32:5). And the Israelites arose early the following day to make sacrifices to this new god.

As a matter of fact, part of Moses' Mount Sinai journey was receiving the Ten Commandments (which Aaron and the rest of the Israelites had heard in Exodus 20). Here's a quick refresher on the first:

> You shall have no other gods before Me. You shall not make for yourself a carved image, or any likeness of anything that is in heaven above, or that is in the earth beneath, or that is in the water under the earth. You shall not bow down to them or serve them, for I the Lord your God am a jealous God, visiting the iniquity of the fathers on the children to the third and the fourth generation of those who hate Me, but showing steadfast love to thousands of those who love Me and keep My commandments. (Exodus 20:3–6)

Oops.

But Aaron didn't even need the Ten Commandments to know how harebrained this plan was. So why did he go through with it?

I think it's because Aaron finally saw an opportunity to one-up his little brother. Moses wasn't around to defend himself, and the people were upset with him. They were looking for new leadership (bonus points for someone who caved to their every desire), and Aaron could be that.

For once, Aaron could be the hero.

I imagine Aaron's thinking played out like the familiar scenario in a classic cartoon: the protagonist has an angel on one shoulder, a devil on the other, each pleading for the human to take their advice. Aaron flicked the angel away, high-fived the devil, and went along with what made the people happy.

This choice did not sit well with God. Sick of the Israelites' stubborn and rebellious nature, God told Moses: "Let Me alone, that My wrath may burn hot against them and I may consume them, in order that I may make a great nation of you" (Exodus 32:10).

Moses desperately pleaded with God and convinced Him not to destroy the Israelites completely (Exodus 32:11–13), but this sin could not pass without consequence. After Moses made his way down the mountain and arrived at the camp, he was so filled with righteous anger that he smashed the tablets containing the Ten Commandments and immediately burned the calf. Moses ground the ashes into a powder, mixed the powder with water, and forced the people to drink it.

Then he gathered the Levites (descendants of Levi who were close to God) and gave them heavy but important instructions from God: they were to go from one end of the camp to the other and kill any worshipers of the calf, even brothers, friends, and neighbors. Three thousand people died that day. However, God still wasn't done. He capped off His punishment with a great plague that crippled the Israelite camp.

Aaron had been so desperate to appease the people that he completely forgot—or ignored—God's divinity. And the very people he sought to please paid the price for it.

In fact, God was so angry with Aaron that it took Moses' pleading prayers to keep God from destroying him (Deuteronomy 9:20).

All because jealous Aaron wanted a little time in the spotlight.

We're called to work for God, not humankind. Colossians 3:23 instructs us, "Whatever you do, work heartily, as for the Lord and not for men." Jesus chided the Pharisees for loving human praise more than praise from God (John 12:43).

The Bible makes it clear that pleasing the world is worth nothing compared to pleasing God, but it's so tempting to chase it. We want affirmation from our peers. We see our co-workers, friends, and family every day, so we want to appease them and earn their respect. We don't physically see or interact with God, so we have the tendency to place human adoration over His.

The boost that comes from human praise is pleasing but fleeting, and we're left chasing more recognition. It is a drink that never truly quenches our thirst.

God's praise is different. When He looks at us and says, "Well done, good and faithful servant" (Matthew 25:21), that praise has lasting impact.

Paul puts it best in his Letter to the Galatians: "For am I now seeking the approval of man, or of God? Or am I trying to please man? If I were still trying to please man, I would not be a servant of Christ" (Galatians 1:10).

For most of his life, Aaron was, on the surface at least, fine with Moses' role as leader. But all those instances of taking the backseat caused a jealousy to fester and grow, and his desire for recognition led to the deaths of thousands.

And yet I'm willing to bet that most days Moses would have happily traded places with his big brother! You think he wanted to be taunted by Pharaoh (Exodus 5:2), or face the Egyptian ruler after the king's son died (Exodus 12:29–31)? How would Aaron have handled the panicked masses as the Egyptian army bore down on them at the Red Sea (Exodus 14:5–20)? Did he really want to deal with the whiny brood of Israelites, who peppered Moses with questions and complaints throughout the entire desert journey?

Moses put up with a great deal, but Aaron had a warped view of his brother's life. For all the authority Moses had, he also had a lot of responsibilities heaped onto him. He led a very difficult life.

Aaron's jealousy attached blinders to his head, allowing him to see only Moses' communion with God and the rare occasions on which the Israelites thanked him. Aaron didn't recognize the awesome opportunity he had been given; he played an important role in the largest rescue mission in human history. Without his bravery and ability to speak to Pharaoh, the entire story might have played out differently.

Aaron's vanity brings to mind Jeremiah 5:21: "Hear this, O foolish and senseless people, who have eyes, but see not, who have ears, but hear not."

He saw God's miracles. He heard Moses declare him as God's chosen high priest (Exodus 28:1–2). But his vanity caused him to forget everything God had done, and the people suffered for it.

You'd think this story would make Aaron a new man, one who never again questioned his place in God's plan.

Not so much.

Skip ahead to Numbers 12. Aaron and Miriam, another older sibling of Moses, criticized their younger brother because he had married a Cushite woman. The Bible reveals, however, that their problem with Moses wasn't due to his choice of wife; it was his standing with the people:

> And they said, "Has the Lord indeed spoken only through Moses? Has He not spoken through us also?" (Numbers 12:2)

Miriam and Aaron used Moses' wife as a smokescreen to try and spread discontent throughout the camp. One slight drawback to this plan: God heard them. And He didn't appreciate this slander.

Miriam was soon struck with leprosy. Leprosy was the sign of the walking dead in biblical times. The flesh of the infected person became white as snow and dotted with disgusting lesions. The way modern media depicts zombies isn't far off from how people with leprosy looked in these times. These scaly individuals were untouchable to society.

At the Lord's instruction, Miriam was kept outside the camp for seven days, when she could return healed.

Aaron's attempts to bring the spotlight to himself had dire consequences for others. When he created the golden calf, thousands of Israelites died, and many more became sick. When he complained about not getting the glory, his sister was struck with a deadly disease.

It can be so difficult to prioritize pleasing God over pleasing humankind. We can see humans. Touch them. Hear them. Bask in their praise. Feel the pain of their rejection.

As important as all that feels now, it's meaningless in the end. Pleasing God affects our eternity; our eighty or so years on earth are just a drop in the bucket in comparison. We must keep 1 John 2:16 top of mind:

> For all that is in the world—the desires of the flesh and the desires of the eyes and pride of life—is not from the Father but is from the world.

Aaron was so focused on how the people viewed him that he forgot how God felt about him. God absolutely adores humans; of all creation, we were the only living beings to be created in His image (Genesis 1:27). When He created the world, He didn't stop after forming the galaxies, creating light, or making animals of all kinds. It was only after He made humans that He deemed His work "very good" (Genesis 1:31) and ceased creating (Genesis 2:3). We were the completion point.

Check out God's promise in Isaiah 54:10:

> "For the mountains may depart and the hills be removed, but My steadfast love shall not depart from you, and My covenant of peace shall not be removed," says the LORD, who has compassion on you.

Nothing—nothing whatsoever—can separate you from God's love. You can kill, steal, worship other gods, and prioritize people over Him. He'll still love you.

Even as Aaron tripped up, God still loved Him. He may have had to lay down some punishment (that's how we learn), but He never stopped loving Aaron.

Aaron probably would have fared far better if he had adopted the mindset of a man that would come generations later: John the Baptist.

John the Baptist

Just about everything about John the Baptist was notable. Consider:

- He was the miracle baby granted to Zechariah and Elizabeth, who had no children and were thought to be far too old to conceive (Luke 1:5–23).
- He was filled with the Holy Spirit while he was still in his mother's womb (Luke 1:66).
- He lived in the wilderness and wore odd clothes woven from camel hair (Matthew 3:3–4).
- He had an incredible speaking ability that drew people from all over the region (Matthew 3:5).
- He was bold enough to call out the hypocrisy of the Pharisees, the religious leaders of the time (Matthew 3:7–10).

Whatever you thought about this man, there was no ignoring him.

Such notoriety easily could have gone to John's head. People were so attracted to his impassioned speeches that they not only traveled miles just to see him but also trusted him to baptize them

(Matthew 3:6). The Jewish leaders felt threatened by John's ministry and attempted to discredit him (John 1:19–28).

John was the superstar. He was everything Aaron wanted to be.

But his mission wasn't to be the leading man. In John 1:8, we're told, "He was not the light, but came to bear witness about the light."

Sounds kind of how God described Aaron, right? Remember "He shall be your mouth" (Exodus 4:16)? John's entire existence, every word he spoke, was to tell of Jesus' coming. This was his purpose.

Think about the role of an opening act at a concert. This is usually an up-and-coming group that doesn't have the fame to attract crowds on their own. Their role is to get the fans excited while they wait for the headliner to take the stage.

John the Baptist was the opening act for Jesus, but people thought he was the star of the show. It would have been human nature to embrace their love and bask in their praise.

But John recoiled from this recognition:

> I baptize you with water for repentance, but He who is coming after me is mightier than I, whose sandals I am not worthy to carry. He will baptize you with the Holy Spirit and fire. (Matthew 3:11)

> I am the voice of one crying out in the wilderness, "Make straight the way of the Lord," as the prophet Isaiah said. (John 1:23)

> The next day he saw Jesus coming toward him, and said, "Behold, the Lamb of God, who takes away the sin of the world! This is He of whom I said, 'After me

> comes a man who ranks before me, because He was before me.'" (John 1:29–30)

John was so humble that when Jesus asked to be baptized by him, John responded, "I need to be baptized by You, and do You come to me?" (Matthew 3:14).

John understood that his moving speeches were not through his own eloquence. They were from God, and he was to use them to glorify his Maker.

His faithfulness ended up costing him his life. John publicly criticized Herod Antipas, the ruler of Galilee, for the wrongs the man had committed. For this he was thrown into prison and eventually beheaded as a party favor (Matthew 14:6–12).

Not exactly the way a superstar would want to go out.

But that's the big takeaway: because John used his great influence to announce Jesus' coming, the Jews were ready to see some fireworks when Jesus arrived. They knew the Savior was on the way, but they were still amazed by the miracles Jesus performed.

That's the beauty of John's humility. Though he didn't get to see the end result, his work resulted in great things. Even as he watched the executioner sharpening his blade, I don't think John ever considered how things might have played out differently.

What if he had accepted the title of hero the crowds wanted to give him?

What if he had allied with the powerful religious leaders rather than put himself in their crosshairs?

What if he had appeased Herod instead of challenging him?

I find it hard to believe these alternate realities even entered John's head. This was a man so consumed by his passion for God that he lived in the wilderness and feasted on locusts (Matthew

3:3–4). I think he did this not only to have stillness and aloneness with God but also to separate himself from the adoring masses and resist the temptations of their praise.

John's life brings to mind my favorite Bible verse, Acts 20:24, in which Paul dropped this humility bomb: "But I do not account my life of any value nor as precious to myself, if only I may finish my course and the ministry that I received from the Lord Jesus, to testify to the gospel of the grace of God."

The Bible has dozens of examples of this selfless mindset. An imprisoned Joseph interpreted Pharaoh's dreams and gave God the glory (Genesis 41). Daniel survived a night in the lions' den and credited God (Daniel 6). Saul gave up a prominent position in the community to become Paul, a vagabond, prisoner, and martyr.

Then there's the ultimate example: Jesus.

Take a moment to consider the power Jesus could have wielded if He chose. He performed miracles. He drove action with His sermons. Adoring crowds flocked just to get a glimpse of Him.

His very presence threatened the religious monopoly created by the Pharisees (Luke 13:17). His power caught the attention of the Roman authorities, and the Jewish Council worried how they would respond (John 11:48).

The Jewish people were convinced that Jesus was a military leader coming to free them from Roman rule (John 6:15). When He arrived in Jerusalem on the week of His crucifixion, crowds lined the streets and laid palm branches down on the path for His arrival.

How did Jesus arrive? Upon a majestic steed, with a protective entourage keeping overzealous fans at bay?

Nope. He came in riding on a donkey, the humblest of beasts.

His companions were not warriors but fishermen, tax collectors, and people cast aside by society.

And His message remained consistent: I'm not the one who matters. God is.

> For I have not spoken on My own authority, but the Father who sent Me has Himself given Me a commandment—what to say and what to speak. (John 12:49)

> And this is eternal life, that they know You, the only true God, and Jesus Christ whom You have sent. (John 17:3)

> I can do nothing on My own. As I hear, I judge, and My judgment is just, because I seek not My own will but the will of Him who sent Me. (John 5:30)

> But the hour is coming, and is now here, when the true worshipers will worship the Father in spirit and truth, for the Father is seeking such people to worship Him. (John 4:23)

Rather than rightly claim His place as ruler of the people, Jesus allowed Himself to be killed by His very creation.

Why?

Because we were dead without Him.

> And being found in human form, He humbled Himself by becoming obedient to the point of death, even death on a cross. (Philippians 2:8)

As Christians, I think we risk becoming numb to the reality of this verse. We've heard John 3:16 so many times we can recite it in our sleep, but do we ever slow down enough to consider what Jesus' sacrifice meant?

Jesus went out in the most shameful way possible. Roman soldiers dressed Him in a purple robe, shoved a crown of thorns on His head, handed Him a stick for a scepter, and mockingly bowed before Him, scoffing at His divinity (Matthew 27:27–29). They beat Him with a reed and spat on Him until they tired of insulting Him (Mark 15:19–20). Jewish guards and priests blindfolded Him and punched Him, challenging, "Prophesy! Who is it that struck You?" (Luke 22:64). As Jesus hung on the cross, slowly suffocating in public view, the soldiers rolled dice for His clothes (Matthew 27:35).

And that was just the Roman soldiers. The priests belittled Him as He died: "He saved others; He cannot save Himself. He is the King of Israel; let Him come down now from the cross, and we will believe in Him" (Matthew 27:42). Both revolutionaries crucified alongside Jesus ridiculed Him (Matthew 27:44). A sign was fastened and hung above His head that mocked Him: "This is the King of the Jews" (Luke 23:38).

Jesus' creation, the very people He came to earth to save, treated Him like dirt. And He took it all without a word of protest (Acts 8:32).

He didn't have to.

Jesus could have come down off the cross and given His children a punishment for the ages. At any time, He could have ascended back to heaven.

But He humbled Himself. He considered Himself below us in order to save us.

Seriously, stop reading for sixty seconds and think about that. Your sins, the ones you committed today, were what pinned Jesus to the cross. He accepted the burden of your sins without protest. In fact, He'd do it again if He had to.

Now *that* is humility.

> For you know the grace of our Lord Jesus Christ, that though He was rich, yet for your sake He became poor, so that you by His poverty might become rich. (2 Corinthians 8:9)

> It shall not be so among you. But whoever would be great among you must be your servant, and whoever would be first among you must be your slave, even as the Son of Man came not to be served but to serve, and to give His life as a ransom for many. (Matthew 20:26–28)

What if Aaron had adopted that mindset? How differently might things have played out for him?

To be very clear, Aaron wasn't a selfish man. He made a lot of sacrifices too, and he received very little fanfare for them. His life is deserving of recognition.

But even as he acted humbly, he held tiny pockets of resentment in his heart that came out at the worst times and had severe consequences.

It's very easy to become jealous of those that receive more acclaim around us. The desire to be first is part of our selfish nature.

We should instead strive for the selflessness that John the Baptist and, more importantly, Jesus embraced. John identified someone more important than himself and acknowledged that this newcomer was his superior.

Jesus knew He was holier and more powerful than the pitiful humans that mocked Him, and yet He humbled Himself to achieve a greater mission that would ultimately prove to be better for all.

Larry Jordan surely felt pangs of jealousy of his brother at times, but he was humble enough to recognize Michael was the superior player.

Yet when asked if Michael's fame bothered him, Larry said it didn't because he knew how hard Michael worked.

You think MJ worked hard. Look at what Jesus did.

Then take Larry's approach, not Aaron's.

CHAPTER 13

WILD LIVING

Do not be conformed to this world, but be transformed by the renewal of your mind, that by testing you may discern what is the will of God, what is good and acceptable and perfect.
(Romans 12:2)

I bet you didn't open this book and expect to read about *Wedding Crashers*, did you?

In fact, I'm willing to bet you could count on one hand (maybe even one finger?) the number of times that movie has been referenced in a sermon or God-centric content. And for good reason: this raunchy, R-rated comedy has enough foul language, sexual innuendos, and scantily-clad women to make Hugh Heffner blush.

But I'm going to break the mold, do something crazy, and see if we can learn something from this movie. It shows just how upside down is society's view toward a wild lifestyle.

Because I cannot in good conscience recommend watching this movie, here's a quick synopsis:

Protagonists Jeremy and John are best friends who use trickery to attend complete strangers' weddings so they can party and have one-night stands with beautiful women. Their behavior is immature and despicable, yet Jeremy and John are portrayed as fun-loving heroes: clever enough to fool the fellow wedding attendees, suave enough to win over any woman, and slick enough to effortlessly get away with whatever they please. They're simply too cool to be caught.

I still remember the first time I saw the movie during a basketball team dinner during my sophomore year of high school. We busted our guts laughing at the jokes and quoted the movie's most memorable lines for weeks. No one said it out loud, but everyone felt the same way: we all wanted to be Jeremy and John.

We didn't necessarily want to fool innocent people or bed as many women as possible (at least, I know I didn't). But the thought of living that carefree lifestyle, of always being the life of the party—that was something we all wanted.

Looking back now, it's easy to see how foolish and childish these thoughts were. Our *Wedding Crashers* heroes had no stakes. Their actions had no consequences. That may sound great, but it's not real.

In real life, the pair would have been caught and kicked out of many of the weddings. One of their one-night stands might have resulted in a pregnancy. Their livers may well have failed due to alcohol consumption.

Carefree, wild living has life-altering repercussions. I bet you can identify specific examples in your life. I know I can.

And so could David.

David

For much of his life, David was a spiritual rock star, one whom God called "a man after My heart" (Acts 13:22). God empowered him to slay the giant Goliath, escape the diligent pursuit of jealous king Saul, pen much of the Psalms, and make Israel the region's dominant nation for most of his forty-year reign. So revered was David that Jesus is often referred to as the "Son of David" in the Bible.

He was kind of a big deal.

Yet through all his successes, David maintained a God-centered mindset. Before big moments, he prayed (1 Samuel 23:2; 2 Samuel 5:19). When he achieved success, he praised God (2 Samuel 7:18–29) and gave Him the credit (1 Chronicles 17:16–27; 29:10–14).

Humble and devoted as he was to God, even David was seduced by the *Wedding Crashers* lifestyle. Though he knew it was wrong, he allowed his human desires to lead him to wild living, with lethal results.

In 2 Samuel 11, we find Israel in a period of great prosperity. The nation had just scored military victories over surrounding nations Moab, Edom, Philistia, and Amalek. The Bible tells us, "The Lord gave victory to David wherever he went" (2 Samuel 8:14). That includes a battle with the Ammonites, whom the Israelites routed and chased back behind the walls of their city. In the spring, David sent the Israelite army to crush the Ammonites once and for all.

One afternoon, David took a stroll atop the rooftop of his palace. As he surveyed the city, he spotted a gorgeous woman bathing on one of the buildings below. Temptation arose, and David sent messengers to find out who she was. The woman was Bathsheba, the wife of Uriah, one of Israel's finest soldiers who was currently in the battle against the Ammonites.

David was well aware how wrong it would be to sleep with any married woman (Leviticus 20:10), much less the wife of a man who was completely loyal to him. God tells us to flee from temptation (2 Timothy 2:22), promising that He'll never give us a temptation too enticing to resist (1 Corinthians 10:13). This doesn't mean enduring in the face of temptation is easy; as I'm sure you can attest to, it's really hard!

Rather than fight temptation, David allowed his eyes to linger on Bathsheba's figure as lust consumed his mind and overtook his rational thoughts. He had Bathsheba brought to his palace, only to learn later that during this one-night stand, she had become pregnant (2 Samuel 11:5).

Oops.

How did this man of God let his morals slip so far? And now she was pregnant. Thanks to David's wild living, the king had a messy situation on his hands. And he was about to make it worse.

The responsible thing would have been for David to come clean, but it would have been painful for everyone involved. The people would look at virtuous King David differently, and he would lose a good deal of respect, especially among the soldiers. Uriah would likely never look at his wife the same way again, and Bathsheba might be viewed as a loose woman who cheated on her husband. Most worrisome of all, the penalty for adultery was death.

So David took a different route. He sent a note to his commander, Joab, to have Uriah return and give him updates on the situation with the Ammonites. But David's motives become clear when we learn he sent Uriah to his own home at the end of the night. David hoped Uriah would take this rare night off to be with his wife, and when Uriah eventually learned that Bathsheba was pregnant, he would assume the baby was his. He would have had no reason to think differently.

Only Uriah didn't comply with David's ploy. He didn't believe he deserved any special treatment not also awarded to his fellow soldiers, all of whom remained in tents without their wives on the battlefield. What had he done to enjoy a night of relaxation when his comrades didn't receive the same? So Uriah slept at the door of the king's house with all the servants of his lord, and Bathsheba slept alone.

"My lord Joab and the servants of my lord are camping in the open field," Uriah explained in 2 Samuel 11:11. "Shall I then go to my house, to eat and to drink and to lie with my wife? As you live, and as your soul lives, I will not do this thing."

Growing more desperate, David kept Uriah around for another night, hosting him at dinner and getting him drunk on wine. But instead of forgoing honor for lust in his inebriated state, Uriah passed out on the couch.

> Whoever walks in integrity walks securely, but he who makes his ways crooked will be found out. (Proverbs 10:9)

David wasn't going to be able to lie his way out of this one. Rather than finally admit his folly, David doubled down in the worst way.

The king sent Uriah back to the battlefield carrying a message for Joab: stick Uriah on the front lines, where the fighting would be the fiercest. When the battle got underway, have the rest of the men withdraw, leaving Uriah alone and exposed on the open battlefield.

David was signing Uriah's death warrant.

This is the same man who twice had the opportunity to kill

Saul when Israel's previous king hunted him without reason in the wilderness (1 Samuel 24; 26:5–10). In the world's eyes, David would have been justified in ending Saul's life. Both times, however, David declined, choosing God's way over what his heart desired.

Now he was doing the complete opposite: sentencing an innocent, virtuous man to a senseless death.

David was also making a stupid maneuver from a tactical standpoint. The Israelites had the Ammonites pinned within their walled city. They had no need to attack; they had formed a perimeter around the city that prevented both escape and the entry of any supplies, food, or water. Eventually, the Ammonites would either starve to death, or they would have to come out from behind their protective walls and fight on open fields, where the Israelites would surely finish them off.

David's order put other men in unnecessary danger, and we learn that at least one other soldier was killed in the needless advance (2 Samuel 11:24). His desire to cover up his wild actions blinded him to other consequences, including the lives of the men who had pledged their lives to fight for him.

Ultimately, David's plan was successful: Uriah was killed, and soon after the Israelites conquered the Ammonites. Once Bathsheba's period of mourning for Uriah concluded, David had her brought to the palace, and he married her. She then gave birth to a son. After a turbulent few weeks, the waves had calmed and the sea was smooth once more.

But not everything was as peachy as it seemed.

David may have fooled others, but God saw his actions and his heart. No matter how buttoned-up and clean a cover-up may look, there's always One who knows the truth.

> For His eyes are on the ways of a man, and He sees all his steps. There is no gloom or deep darkness where evildoers may hide themselves. (Job 34:21–22)

Through the prophet Nathan, God informed David that his misadventures would not go unpunished. This was no *Wedding Crashers* tale, in which the friends escaped the tricky situation unscathed. No, there was going to be quite a bit of pain here.

In 2 Samuel 12:10–12, Nathan informed David:

- "The sword shall never depart from your house" (verse 10). Indeed, David's offspring were violent and ever at odds (2 Samuel 13:1–17, 26–30; 1 Kings 2:23–25).
- "I will raise up evil against you out of your own house" (verse 11). Absalom, one of David's sons, tried to overthrow his father (2 Samuel 15:10–16).
- "I will take your wives before your eyes and give them to your neighbor, and he shall lie with your wives in the sight of this sun. For you did it secretly, but I will do this thing before all Israel and before the sun" (verses 11–12). While David was hiding from him, Absalom set up a tent on the palace roof in plain view and slept with his father's concubines (2 Samuel 16:15–22).

Mortified by these revelations, David finally confessed, "I have sinned against the Lord" (2 Samuel 12:13).

No kidding.

That's about as surprising as Jason Voorhees (from *Friday the 13th*) admitting, "I might have a slight problem with violence."

Then God (through Nathan) said, "The Lord also has put away your sin; you shall not die. Nevertheless, because by this deed you have utterly scorned the LORD, the child who is born to you shall die" (2 Samuel 12:13–14).

God forgave David and wouldn't put him to death for his abhorrent behavior. But David wouldn't walk away from his actions scot-free either.

David was repentant as could be. He pleaded with God to spare the child. He refused to eat and lay all night on the bare ground. The combination of love for his child and guilt that the child's death was his fault wrung his stomach into knots.

Even though the Lord loved him, David still had to live with the fallout of his sin. His wild living had consequences, and the child died of illness.

And David's life would never be the same again. All the Lord's other promises came to pass as his kingdom began to unravel. His sons and daughters warred both with one another and him, and the entire country was in jeopardy until Solomon (David's second child with Bathsheba) took the wheel.

No doubt David was indeed a great man who did incredible things for God's kingdom. He's arguably one of the three or four most important characters in the Bible.

Yet when he let his morals slip and pursued his earthly desires, everything fell apart on him. Worse yet, he didn't know when to stop. Rather than admit his failure, he kept doubling down on his poor choices. He was like the Incredible Hulk when Bruce Banner turned green: he rampaged at will, and only when he was truly humbled did he pause long enough to look around and realize all the damage he had done.

God still loved this wild version of David, but He needed to straighten this king out.

Now I don't know you, dear reader, but I imagine it might be hard to relate to David. David started off his life on fire for God. Through David's dangerous experiences, God demonstrated His faithfulness, and David's faith grew. We see David display incredible faith as a youth, then stumble as life went on.

But maybe you come from the opposite direction: you began with a carefree attitude and a life of wild living, and only now are you realizing that you need to slow down and get your priorities in order.

The Prodigal Son

Anytime you think you have been rebellious against God, I want you to turn to Luke 15:11–24. Here we see Jesus tell the story of the ultimate partygoer, an arrogant boy who gambled his life away. At the end, the world saw no worth in him.

And yet, his story ends in redemption and rejoicing.

In Luke 15, Jesus taught the Jewish religious leaders about why He associated with tax collectors and sinners. He introduced the concept with two short stories, one about a shepherd recovering a lost sheep and the second about a woman searching long and hard for a lost silver coin. These tales are warm-ups for the main act: the parable of the prodigal son.

In Jesus' parable, we're introduced to a man with two sons. Both sons would receive a portion of their father's estate when he died; the older would get two-thirds, the younger one-third (Deuteronomy 21:17).

Only the younger son didn't want to wait to get his cash. He was sick of what he believed was a waste of his life at home, so he said, "Father, give me the share of property that is coming to me" (Luke 15:12).

Some kid, right?

He basically told his dad, "Look, I don't want to wait around for you to die, so can you just give me my money so I can get out of here?"

Can you imagine if you said that to your father? I don't know about you, but I'm far more likely to leave that conversation with a pair of busted eardrums than my inheritance.

Yet the father agreed, and a few days later the younger son packed up everything and moved away to a distant land, likely with little intention of ever seeing his merciful father again. And he partied hard. The Bible doesn't specify what he spent his money on, but use your imagination. Travel. Booze. Gambling. Women. Extravagant meals. This young man had no sense of reality; his dad had always footed the bill for him before. What was money to him?

After the son squandered everything on "reckless living" (Luke 11:13), a famine arose in the land, and he began to starve. So desperate was the youngster that he took a job feeding pigs, and he was so hungry that even the pig's food became a juicy cheeseburger or rack of ribs in his eyes. But "no one gave him anything" (verse 16).

As bleak as the son's situation appears on the surface, his shame goes even deeper. According to Moses' Law, pigs were unclean animals (Leviticus 11:7–8, Deuteronomy 14:8), so the Jews weren't supposed to eat them or use them as sacrifices. To minimize the risk of sullying themselves, most Jews avoided even touching swine. For this son to stoop not only to feeding them but also to desiring to steal their food, meant that he had truly hit rock bottom.

And where were his friends? The last time I checked, it's pretty hard to party alone. I imagine he had drinking buddies, gambling parties, and women to pleasure him. But when his money ran out and he wasn't fun anymore, he lost all value to them, and they wanted nothing to do with him. They didn't care that he waded in pig muck to survive. He was as good as dead to them.

Amid the sludge and slime, the man had a realization: even the servants at his father's house were well-fed. They lived far better lives than he currently did. He decided he should return home: not with hope of reconciliation but of survival. The son had awoken to the disservice he had done to his father and didn't expect a warm welcome.

However, if he came forward humbly and offered himself as a slave, perhaps his father would take him on as a hired servant. It would be terribly embarrassing, of course, but at least he wouldn't be dying of hunger and drooling over the pig slop.

With his tail firmly tucked between his legs, the young son returned home. I'm certain he rehearsed the coming meeting with his father in his head hundreds of times on the journey, again and again playing over what he would say and how his father might react. When his home finally came into view, I can almost see the son, grimy and clothed in tattered shreds, exhaling a deep breath and muttering, "Here goes nothing."

He never could have expected what came next.

> But while he was still a long way off, his father saw him and felt compassion, and ran and embraced him and kissed him. And the son said to him, "Father, I have sinned against heaven and before you. I am no longer worthy to be called your son." But the father

> said to his servants, "Bring quickly the best robe, and put it on him, and put a ring on his hand, and shoes on his feet. And bring the fattened calf and kill it, and let us eat and celebrate. For this my son was dead, and is alive again; he was lost, and is found." And they began to celebrate. (Luke 15:20–24)

Wait, what?

This rebellious, good-for-nothing son had essentially spat in his dad's face. And yet his father rejoiced at his return. He not only welcomed his son home, but he also spent even more resources to celebrate the return of this rebel. The father's behavior is nonsensical yet admirable.

I can see the skeptic out there saying, "Awesome. That's a great story. But it's not real, so what does it have to do with my life?"

The story is 100 percent true, and you play one of the main characters. You are the rebellious son, and God is the father.

God provided you an incredible existence. You could live your life needing nothing, always satiated, well-fed, and happy. But you wanted more. You thought the world had more to offer than God was showing you.

You chose reckless living—sin—over God's blessings and promises. You took the future in heaven He promised you and spent it on the fleeting pleasures of this world. You wasted your inheritance on wild living until you had nothing left. Ashamed and broken, you crawled back to God, desperate for any semblance of recognition, much less reconciliation.

But look at God's response. I want to dig a bit deeper into Scripture to drive home a few points here:

- "But while he was still a long way off, his father saw him" (verse 20). The father spent some time outdoors each day, surveying the outskirts of his property and hoping that his beloved son would reappear.
- "And [he] felt compassion, and ran and embraced him and kissed him" (verse 20). I cannot imagine how hurt this father was when his son left him. This life that he had created, that he had loved, nurtured, and raised, had openly rejected and left him. Yet there's no trace of bitterness in the father's response. He didn't wait; at the first sign of his son's return, he pursued him.
- "And the son said to him, 'Father, I have sinned against heaven and before you. I am no longer worthy to be called your son.' But the father said to his servants, 'Bring quickly the best robe'" (verses 21–22). The father asked for nothing in return. He doesn't ask for his money back, and when his son offers some method of repayment, he doesn't even acknowledge it. His focus is solely on the celebration.

God's love goes so far beyond our understanding. The father's actions in this tale make little sense until we acknowledge that God loves us more than we can even comprehend.

> "For the mountains may depart and the hills be removed, but My steadfast love shall not depart from you, and My covenant of peace shall not be removed," says the Lord, who has compassion on you. (Isaiah 54:10)

Your entire world can crumble around you, and yet God will still love you. No amount of disdain you show toward Him can affect the way He feels about you. He will never leave you or forsake you, no matter how far you stray from the perfect path He has laid out for you (Deuteronomy 31:6).

When God sees you timidly approaching home, He will run to you. He will embrace you. He will show you more love and wonders than you can imagine.

But at this point we need to acknowledge a very important part of Jesus' parable: the father didn't chase down his son.

When the son asked for his inheritance, the father didn't argue. As the son packed his bags, the father didn't plead for him to stay. And after the son left, the father didn't try to track him down or send any kind of communication.

He let his son go.

This doesn't mean that the father didn't care about his son; quite the opposite! I'm willing to bet the father lost all kinds of sleep thinking of his wayward kid. He may have developed an ulcer with worry. But he didn't interfere.

He loved his son enough to let him make his own decision. And while he hoped and prayed that he would see his son again, he wasn't going to force him to return, even as he knew his son was making the biggest mistake of his life.

So it is with you and God. When you choose sin, you're the wild rebel that leaves your Father's trusted side. He knows this is a bad move for you in the long run, but He's going to let you make that mistake.

Why? Let's try to imagine if the parable had played out slightly differently.

What if the father had denied his son the inheritance and kept him at home? While he would have the peace of mind that his son was safe, the boy would (at least temporarily) resent him.

What if, after a few weeks, the father sent out a search party to find his boy and bring him home? The youth would have been furious, and a deep chasm of broken trust would have threatened their relationship forever.

No, the only way for the boy to truly realize his mistakes, recognize all the good things his father had in store for him, and repent was for him to come to the conclusion himself. It was a lesson his dad couldn't force upon him.

In the same way, God lets us make our mistakes. He lets us take our inheritance and run away. And while you're gone, He won't try to force His way back into your life.

But once the fun of wild living wears off and you find yourself in the pig pen, He'll always be waiting, watching that horizon as His Spirit works through the Word and the Sacraments to bring you back in repentance. And when you do, He throws His finest robes on you and kills the fattened calf. "For this my son was dead, and is alive again; he was lost, and is found" (Luke 15:24).

The father's words sound very similar to how Paul describes our relationship with Christ:

> Now if we have died with Christ, we believe that we will also live with Him. (Romans 6:8)

> Therefore, if anyone is in Christ, he is a new creation. The old has passed away; behold, the new has come. (2 Corinthians 5:17)

> I have been crucified with Christ. It is no longer I who live, but Christ who lives in me. And the life I now live in the flesh I live by faith in the Son of God, who loved me and gave Himself for me. (Galatians 2:20)

Death to life.

Because of Jesus' sacrifice, there is no barrier between you and God. There is no shame in your return. There is no judgment on His behalf.

Jesus cleared the path for your return with His sacrifice (John 3:16). Now the only thing separating you from God is yourself.

In *Wedding Crashers*, Jeremy and John have a set of rules when it applies to crashing weddings. Most of these are, as you'd expect, pretty reprehensible. I do think it's worth noting the first rule, however: never leave a friend behind.

That's how Jesus felt about you. You deserved to be left behind, penniless and dining with swine.

But Jesus didn't leave you behind. And because of His sacrifice, you have a boatload of forgiveness and an eternity in heaven waiting for you.

CHAPTER 14

WORRY

And which of you by being anxious
can add a single hour to his span of life?
(Matthew 6:27)

As my thirteen-year-old self limped off the basketball court in the fall of 2007, I wasn't worried about adding an hour to my life. I just hoped to add a few more minutes to my quickly-evaporating basketball career.

Up until that point, I had always assumed basketball was my special skill. My dad had played in the NBA, and I was one of the tallest kids in my class. I had never tried out for any AAU (Amateur Athletic Union) or select teams, but I was generally one of the better players on my YMCA and intramural squads. When tryouts for the eighth-grade team came around, I knew I wasn't the best. But I figured I was a shoo-in at least to make the team.

Wow, was I wrong.

Those two days humbled me in ways I hadn't previously experienced. The poor rims at Kiewit Middle School needed reconstructive surgery after being assaulted by my jump shot. Quicker players ran circles around me and my lead feet, and my poor conditioning had me gasping for breath after a couple of trips down the court.

I was completely unprepared for this challenge, and as I left the gym with my fate hanging in the balance, I had to consider for the first time in my life that I was not a good basketball player. I had entered tryouts thinking I'd be on the vaunted A team. Now I was just hoping to squeak onto the B squad.

The very thought filled me with worry. What would people say?

"Dan's dad played in the NBA, and he can't even make his eighth-grade team?"

"What is all that height good for anyway?" (I was, and still am, six feet six inches tall.)

"He says he loves the game; I guess that was all just talk."

Fear consumed my body and made sleep that night a hopeless pipe dream. It wasn't until 4:00 p.m. the following day that I nervously arrived at the bulletin board with the tryout results and saw *Daniel Hoppen* among the final names. Relief cascaded over me as I allowed myself to breathe truly normally for the first time in twenty-four hours.

Truth be told, I was right to be concerned about making that team (more on that later). I didn't deserve it. But my fear was not going to decide whether I was a member of the Kiewit Colts or an ashamed spectator in the grandstand.

God would.

Worry is among the most worthless human emotions, and with perspective, it's often easy to see that. The Bible constantly reminds us that worry is folly; these are but a few examples:

> Do not be anxious about anything, but in everything by prayer and supplication with thanksgiving let your requests be made known to God. And the peace of

> God, which surpasses all understanding, will guard your hearts and your minds in Christ Jesus. (Philippians 4:6–7)

> And we know that for those who love God all things work together for good, for those who are called according to His purpose. (Romans 8:28)

> God is our refuge and strength, a very present help in trouble. Therefore we will not fear though the earth gives way, though the mountains be moved into the heart of the sea, though its waters roar and foam, though the mountains tremble at its swelling. (Psalm 46:1–3)

All these verses make so much sense upon examining past worries. I have at my back the God who created the universe. "Whom shall I fear?" (Psalm 27:1).

So why do those awesome promises seem so powerless in the moment, when fear seizes us and everything seems hopeless?

If anyone can relate to irrational worry, it's Saul.

Saul

Physically imposing and stunningly handsome (1 Samuel 9:2), Saul was the obvious choice on paper to serve as Israel's first king. But beneath the shiny veneer, he was an emotional wreck who constantly doubted both himself and God.

It goes without saying that things didn't end well.

A quick refresher: when the Israelites failed to take full ownership of the Promised Land, they continually turned to false gods, so angering God that He actively fought against them in battle

(Judges 2:11–15). But because God had compassion for His chosen people, He raised up a line of judges. While these men and women were far from perfect, they (for the most part) provided direction from God while ensuring their Creator was acknowledged as Israel's leader.

But the Israelites desired a human ruler. They saw the way neighboring nations served monarchs who could create laws and dictate the army according to their needs (as if God didn't know those). So Israel's elders went to Samuel, the current judge and one of the nation's famous prophets, and demanded a human king. A distressed Samuel presented the request to God, who replied, "Obey the voice of the people in all that they say to you, for they have not rejected you, but they have rejected Me from being king over them" (1 Samuel 8:7).

Let's pause briefly and imagine God's pain in this moment. The Israelites had no reason to doubt His goodness or leadership. Not only had God delivered them from generations of slavery in Egypt, but He had also provided sustenance in their journey across the desert (Exodus 16). He had weathered their sinful ways and overcome His frustration, eventually delivering them to the Promised Land. He had even provided a great human leader in Samuel.

And still it wasn't enough. He was rejected by His chosen nation, the ones He treated with more compassion and love than they could even imagine.

Yet, rather than force His people to love Him, He gave them their way. Though He knew the decision was folly, He loved them that much.

We can't miss this point; it's too important. God is our Creator. He determined everything about you; if He wanted, He could influence your every move.

But He doesn't want an army of adoring robots. He wants to be loved back, and love is an active choice. Forced love feels hollow and empty, and that's why God will never make you choose Him. It's His ultimate desire and His primary goal. He works through His powerful Word and Sacrament to create and sustain that faith. But He wants that love to be your decision. Your choice will impact your future.

That leads us back to Saul.

The man had leadership chops, to be sure. He was a talented warrior (1 Samuel 11:1–13) who found success at nearly every turn early in his reign (1 Samuel 14:47–48).

But he was also a serial worrier who was constantly undermined by his lack of confidence. He went missing during his inauguration ceremony as king, only to be found hiding among some nearby baggage (1 Samuel 10:21–23). I can only wonder if the Israelites had some doubts about him in that moment.

Saul's doubt constantly undermined his strengths during his time as king. He panicked in a battle against the Philistines and disobeyed a direct order from Samuel (1 Samuel 13:8–14). Then he boisterously did the same with a directive from God (1 Samuel 15:1–9). Saul also benched himself and allowed a teenage boy with no military experience to take on the Philistines' most powerful warrior one-on-one (1 Samuel 17).

Time and time again, Saul's worry caused him to act rashly and display false bravado that was displeasing to God.

God gave Saul every opportunity to succeed. He aided Saul in battle (1 Samuel 11:6) and allowed him to reign for many years, continually displaying that when Saul obeyed, things went well for him. But Saul just couldn't get the message; time and time again, he chose to worry about what people thought of him (1 Samuel 18:6–8) over what God desired.

In the end, Saul left God no choice but to take Israel back from him. Leaving this brash, uneven man in charge put the entire nation at risk. And in David, God already had a much more suitable replacement waiting in the wings.

Through Samuel, God informed Saul of the penalty of his misdeeds:

> You have done foolishly. You have not kept the command of the LORD your God, with which He commanded you. For then the LORD would have established your kingdom over Israel forever. But now your kingdom shall not continue. The LORD has sought out a man after His own heart, and the LORD has commanded him to be prince over His people, because you have not kept what the LORD commanded you. (1 Samuel 13:13–4)

Saul remained in power for a while longer as David grew and matured into the king Israel needed. But Saul's worry drove him to make mistake after mistake, further distancing himself from God. He disobeyed instructions (1 Samuel 15:1–9) and was impulsive (1 Samuel 14:24–30), fearful (1 Samuel 17:11), and brutally cruel, even to his own son (1 Samuel 20:30–34). The multitude of sins became too painful for God to bear. "I regret that I have made Saul king, for he has turned back from following Me and has not performed My commandments," He told Samuel (1 Samuel 15:11), before ultimately leaving the distrusting king (1 Samuel 16:14).

Saul's worry and fear made an all-powerful, all-knowing God express regret. Really think about that for a second. God promised Saul that his line could reign over His kingdom forever, and all he had to do was believe in the goodness of God, who had never let him down.

But Saul lived in constant fear of attack from all sides. He didn't trust God to deliver victory over his enemies. He viewed David as a threat and tried to kill him on multiple occasions (1 Samuel 18:10–11; 19:9–10) before forcing his ally to go on the run. He even hurled a spear at Jonathan, his blameless son, because Saul thought Jonathan was helping David (1 Samuel 20:33). Saul's anxiety made him an irrational pessimist who acted on every fearful impulse. In the end, as Israel lost a battle against the Philistines, an injured Saul took his own life by falling on his sword rather than be captured, tortured, and executed (1 Samuel 31).

So much promise and potential. Yet what Saul is chiefly remembered for is disappointment.

It's critical to recognize that Saul got plenty of chances. This was not a one-and-done situation. From the very beginning, as Saul cowered among some traveler's extra sandals and toiletries, God could have pulled the plug.

Instead, He empowered Saul. We see many occasions when the Holy Spirit rushed upon a biblical hero, giving people such as Gideon (Judges 6:34) and Samson (Judges 14:6; 14:19; 15:14) the courage and strength to defeat their enemies. This same Spirit once "rushed upon Saul" (1 Samuel 11:6), driving him to muster a massive army and defeat the Ammonites.

Ultimately, Saul could blame his downfall on nothing but his own worry. After Saul's many bouts of doubt, we see the Holy Spirit leave Saul, only to be replaced by a tormenting spirit (1 Samuel 16:14). When adversity arises via Goliath and the Philistines in the next chapter, Saul was "dismayed and greatly afraid" (1 Samuel 17:11). The Spirit that had driven him to great victories before was gone. It instead entered David (1 Samuel 16:13), who displayed more courage than any in the Israelite army and slayed the giant Goliath.

To be clear, worry is not a harbinger of disaster in God's eyes. Naomi feared she was useless and that God had "gone out against" her (Ruth 1:13). God used her daughter-in-law Ruth to establish Jesus' line.

Moses feared he would be killed if he returned to Egypt (Exodus 4:13). God used his actions to free the Israelites from bondage.

Jesus' disciples feared that their Teacher couldn't protect them from a storm at sea (Mark 4:35–40). He not only kept them safe but also used them to change the world.

God just doesn't appreciate being doubted, and can you blame Him? Recall the last time someone didn't trust you to hold up your end of the bargain. Lack of faith, especially from someone you love, cuts deep.

Of course, living a completely carefree existence isn't the right answer either. You can't just assume that God will always deliver your every request on a silver platter; there are going to be times He says no.

And that's a good thing! God doesn't decline your requests because He has a personal vendetta against you; just the opposite, in fact. Unlike us, He can see the entire picture, and He has our best interest in mind (Psalm 121:7–8). It just might not always seem like it in the moment.

In those moments, worry isn't the answer.

Prayer is.

Jehoshaphat

Jehoshaphat was far from perfect. This king of Judah made his fair share of mistakes, allowing idolatry to permeate the land during his rule and allying with the evil Ahab, then the king of Israel, against God's judgment.

But when the cards were stacked against him, Jehoshaphat turned his worry over to God. Lo and behold, God came through.

We pick up the king's story in 2 Chronicles 20. The armies of surrounding nations, the Moabites, Ammonites, and Meunites, declared war on Judah. Messengers arrived to inform Jehoshaphat that this alliance was already at Hazazon-tamar, only about twenty-five miles southeast of Jerusalem, giving the king precious little time to prep for the coming onslaught.

First reaction: worry.

"Then Jehoshaphat was afraid" (2 Chronicles 20:3).

Of course, he should be afraid! Though Judah clearly had a capable military (2 Chronicles 17:10–19), it was no match for this coming horde. The nation was staring extinction in the face.

A little worry is understandable.

But what happens next is extraordinary. Jehoshaphat's fear doesn't even last until the end of the sentence.

> Then Jehoshaphat was afraid and set his face to seek the Lord, and proclaimed a fast throughout all Judah. And Judah assembled to seek help from the

> Lord; from all the cities of Judah they came to seek the Lord. (2 Chronicles 20:3–4)

Look at that. Jehoshaphat knew he couldn't win this battle alone (2 Chronicles 20:12) and immediately pivoted to prayer. The entire nation fasted as their king pleaded with God to deliver them.

As Jehoshaphat prayed, the Spirit of the Lord came upon one of the men and spoke through him:

> Listen, all Judah and inhabitants of Jerusalem and King Jehoshaphat: Thus says the Lord to you, "Do not be afraid and do not be dismayed at this great horde, for the battle is not yours but God's. Tomorrow go down against them. Behold, they will come up by the ascent of Ziz. You will find them at the end of the valley, east of the wilderness of Jeruel. You will not need to fight in this battle. Stand firm, hold your position, and see the salvation of the Lord on your behalf, O Judah and Jerusalem." Do not be afraid and do not be dismayed. Tomorrow go out against them, and the Lord will be with you. (2 Chronicles 20:15–17)

"The battle is not yours but God's."

Wouldn't it be nice always to recall that friendly reminder in times of crisis? Our battles aren't our own. Daunting as the struggle may seem, our enemy simply cannot overwhelm us! Our general not only created the enemy but also knows its very weakness. More importantly, He created us, and He knows how to use our strengths (and the abilities of those around us) to help us through any situation.

Still, Jehoshaphat and his warriors had to be scratching their heads a bit as they turned in for the night; what did God mean, "You will not need to fight in this battle" (verse 17)? Were they supposed to expect this massive force just to surrender?

God had even better plans.

When Judah showed up, all they found were the dead bodies of their enemies. The other armies had turned on and attacked one another, leaving a field of corpses instead of an insurmountable force waiting for God's people. It took Jehoshaphat and his men three days to collect all the plunder from the scene, and the episode put the fear of God into the surrounding nations. Judah lived in peace for the rest of Jehoshaphat's reign.

Allow these tales of two kings to serve as a lesson. In trying times, Saul crumpled so badly that he made God feel remorse (1 Samuel 15:11). Meanwhile, Jehoshaphat "held fast to the Lord" (2 Kings 18:6), trusted Him, and experienced both peace and success.

Take a moment to consider the humble sparrow. In comparison to bald eagles and hawks, sparrows are pretty ordinary creatures, right? Sure, they can fly, but they're so common. There's nothing truly special about them.

Lilies are the plant version of sparrows. While they can be beautiful, they're one of the most common flowers in the world. Though there are many varieties, you can easily purchase them at your local grocery store for a few bucks. They're not exactly a luxury item.

Yet look at Matthew 6:26–34:

> Look at the birds of the air: they neither sow nor reap nor gather into barns, and yet your heavenly Father

> feeds them. Are you not of more value than they? And which of you by being anxious can add a single hour to his span of life?
>
> And why are you anxious about clothing? Consider the lilies of the field, how they grow: they neither toil nor spin, yet I tell you, even Solomon in all his glory was not arrayed like one of these. But if God so clothes the grass of the field, which today is alive and tomorrow is thrown into the oven, will He not much more clothe you, O you of little faith?
>
> Therefore do not be anxious, saying, "What shall we eat?" or "What shall we drink?" or "What shall we wear?" For the Gentiles seek after all these things, and your heavenly Father knows that you need them all. But seek first the kingdom of God and His righteousness, and all these things will be added to you.
>
> Therefore do not be anxious about tomorrow, for tomorrow will be anxious for itself. Sufficient for the day is its own trouble.

You have the chance to grasp the point that Saul never could—God's got this. Life isn't always going to be perfect. That's the consequence of sin.

But when things go badly, you have the God of angel armies at your back. He can defeat your greatest foe without you even having to raise your sword.

Jesus proved this by beating back Satan with nothing but a few words and an iron will.

At the very beginning of His ministry, before He was a household name, Jesus went into the wilderness. Fresh from being baptized by John the Baptist, Jesus was "full of the Holy Spirit" (Luke 4:1). He would need every bit of that strength for what was coming.

He fasted for the next forty days, eating nothing and seeing no one. The devil was also present, a nagging thorn in Jesus' side. As Jesus became hungry and weak, the devil tempted Him in the following ways:

- Food and physical possessions: "If You are the Son of God, command these stones to become loaves of bread" (Matthew 4:3).
- Power: "Then the devil took Him to the holy city and set Him on the pinnacle of the temple and said to Him, 'If You are the Son of God, throw Yourself down, for it is written, "He will command His angels concerning you," and "On their hands they will bear you up, lest you strike your foot against a stone"'" (Matthew 4:5–6).
- Pride: "Again, the devil took Him to a very high mountain and showed Him all the kingdoms of the world and their glory. And he said to Him, 'All these I will give You, if You will fall down and worship me'" (Matthew 4:8–9).

These situations could have given Jesus reasons to worry. His physical state was declining, and any food—even a simple loaf of bread—would have been like a full spread at a three-star restaurant. The second two temptations could cause worry too. Thanks to Adam and Eve's fall (Genesis 3), Satan had some dominion on earth. Maybe Jesus needed to prove His power to get Satan to back off. Or perhaps He should even give in to the devil to gain more influence on his turf.

Yet even in His weakened state, Jesus batted away Satan's pitiful attempts like a cow's tail swats a gnat:

- "It is written, 'Man shall not live by bread alone, but by every word that comes from the mouth of God'" (Matthew 4:4).
- "Again it is written, 'You shall not put the Lord your God to the test'" (Matthew 4:7).
- "Be gone, Satan! For it is written, 'You shall worship the Lord your God and Him only shall you serve'" (Matthew 4:10).

Jesus didn't allow worry about His physical state or His power or status outside of heaven to dictate His response (1 John 2:15). He clung to the promises of His Father, a force against which the devil stood no chance. After being rebuffed for a third time, Satan gave up and left, and angels arrived and cared for Jesus. Then He began calling the apostles and set His ministry in motion.

Pretty great story, right? Before Jesus had any status on earth, the devil tried to gain dominion over Him. But our God was too powerful and smart for these tricks and sent Satan packing.

But what was Jesus doing in the desert in the first place?

> Then Jesus was led up by the Spirit into the wilderness to be tempted by the devil. (Matthew 4:1)

Come again? The Holy Spirit willingly led Jesus into a difficult situation to be tempted by His most powerful enemy?

Seems like a poor battle strategy.

Therein lies the cunning of Jesus' battle tactics. In order to understand what humans go through, He wanted to feel their pain. The pangs of hunger. The desire for power. The temptation of glory. He wanted to feel worry, to be tested (Hebrews 4:15).

Thus, the Holy Spirit led Jesus right into Satan's waiting trap. He had to undo the damage Adam did when he and Eve gave in to Satan all those years ago: "For as by the one man's disobedience the many were made sinners, so by the one man's obedience the many will be made righteous" (Romans 5:19).

It wasn't easy, but Jesus turned this opportunity to worry into a statement to Satan: He was a force to be reckoned with.

Watch out. The Savior had arrived.

Back to my basketball tryout. On the first day of practice, one of the assistant coaches, Mr. Rhodes, pulled me aside. I had a good relationship with Rhodes, who had been my football coach the previous year. A 106-pound beanpole, I had been the smallest player on the team. But through sheer determination and grit, I had grown from the team's weak spot into a valuable contributor and starting cornerback at the end of the season.

"Listen to me, son," Mr. Rhodes said sternly, but with care. "The only reason you're on this team is because of what I saw from you in football last year. Your tryout was bad. The other coaches didn't think you should make it. But the effort you showed in football makes me believe you'll do the same here. I stuck my neck out for you. Don't make me sorry I did that."

And just like that, my confidence was back. I knew I hadn't deserved my spot; better players were cut in favor of me. But I had an advocate at my back who had fought and would continue to fight for me.

Now I would fight for him.

In hindsight, I can see how that conversation changed not only my basketball career but also my life. I worked my butt off after that, shooting for hours after practice each day, running in sand pits in school playgrounds during the summer, consistently being one of the last players to leave the weight room in high school. I was never a star, but I did improve enough to earn a scholarship at a tiny NIAA college before I hung up my sneakers for good.

All because Mr. Rhodes turned my worry into determination.

And Mr. Rhodes was a gym teacher. God is the all-powerful Creator who knows the past, present, and future of your life. If He cares for birds and flowers, won't He show up for you? You can definitely trust Him. Just keep the focus on Christ and not yourself, as Jehoshaphat did.

Don't worry if you throw up some bricks in the tryout. You're going to miss. Just keep plugging ahead and work harder. That same Spirit that at times empowered Gideon, Samson, David, Jehoshaphat, and many others now lives within you (Romans 8:9). Through the Word and Sacraments, He will take away your fear and empower you to do more than you could imagine.

Conclusion

The summer after I turned sixteen, my parents bought me my first car. Two weeks later, it was on the side of the road with its hood in the shape of a tent.

And it was my fault.

My parents had entrusted me with a beautiful white Nissan Maxima that, while not brand-new (my parents were far too wise to buy a sixteen-year-old boy a new car), was in very good shape. I was proud to drive it and show it off to my friends.

That fact made my failure all the more crushing.

One summer morning, on the way to a basketball team weight-lifting session, I pulled out of our neighborhood as I had done dozens of times before with one of my parents in the passenger seat. But on this day, the line at a nearby stoplight had backed up, and before I knew it, my hood was colliding with the trunk of the car in front of me.

Fortunately, no one was injured. In fact, the damage to the car I hit was extremely minimal, and the other driver was very sympathetic and kind. Yet as we waited on the side of the road for the police and my parents to arrive, I couldn't help but look at my triangular mess of a hood and think my life was over.

Dramatic as that might seem in hindsight, I felt very hopeless in the moment. I could only imagine how furious my parents would be that their idiot kid had already managed to trash his new car. How much would repairs cost? Could we even repair it, or was the car totaled? And I had managed to get a ticket (for following too closely) while the ink was still drying on my driver's license. What did that say about my future?

I had made mistakes before, but not anything with long-term repercussions such as this. In my mind, there was no coming back from my failure.

How many times have you felt that way? That you had messed up in an irrevocable way, and no turnaround could save your skin?

Thankfully, God doesn't see you like that.

If you've learned anything from this book, I hope that God's mercy is one of the top takeaways. Even the Bible's greatest heroes stumbled. We all mess up; it's a trademark of sinful humanity. Ever since Adam and Eve took a bite of the fruit and introduced sin into the world, we were assured our share of fender benders.

I've had more than my fair share. Among the highlights:

- I've been laid off twice.
- I failed Eve (page 91) as a dog owner.
- I've had falling outs that cost me multiple friendships.
- I've made my wife cry more times than I care to admit.

I specifically remember one day in 2019 when it felt like my world had finally collapsed on me. I had been unemployed for several months, and though Sarah was fully supporting me, I felt awful relying on her to cover all our expenses.

I felt useless and broken.

On this particular day, I stepped out of the shower and looked in the mirror. I had never felt lower. I became overwhelmed with emotion at my reflection, and tears immediately welled up in my eyes. As I began to weep, I thought to myself, "God, how can You love me? I'm worthless."

Then I heard this voice: "Are you kidding Me? Worthless? You're amazing! I love you so much, and I have big things coming. Just wait to see what I can do."

Suddenly, my sobbing stopped. The voice wasn't audible; it was in my head. Yet the thought hadn't come from my brain; I was too buried in self-pity to muster a thought that positive.

This was the Holy Spirit.

I'm fully willing to admit that I don't deserve a second chance. When I look at all the wrongs I've committed, I wouldn't blame God one bit for looking at me and saying, "I've given that guy so many opportunities. But he just doesn't get it, and I have seven billion other people to look after. He had his chances. I'm moving on."

But He hasn't said that, and He never will.

"I have loved you with an everlasting love; therefore I have continued My faithfulness to you" (Jeremiah 31:3).

Everlasting love. Unfailing love.

> Give thanks to the God of heaven, for His steadfast love endures forever. (Psalm 136:26)

Love endures forever.

> But God, being rich in mercy, because of the great love with which He loved us, even when we were dead in our trespasses, made us alive together with Christ. (Ephesians 2:4–5)

Rich in mercy. He gave us life.

No matter what you do or how worthless you feel, God will

never give up on you. He possesses a love beyond our wildest imagination. He will forgive your worst offenses. Like the father of the prodigal son, He's always watching the horizon, hoping you'll come home. And when He sees you, He comes running with arms extended, wanting nothing from you.

He just wants you.

In His love, He'll show you you're not worthless. Since that day in front of the mirror, here's what's happened in my life:

- I self-published my first book, *God's Broken Heroes*, which encouraged the wonderful Concordia Publishing House to allow me to write a second.
- I not only found a new job but also took on leadership roles there.
- I have a podcast that helps chefs and restaurateurs tell their story and shines the spotlight on their restaurants.
- I, while making all kinds of mistakes, am still the husband to the most beautiful, caring, wonderful wife on this earth.

If God can forgive and empower this unemployed loser, what can He do for you?

I don't know where life finds you as you read these final words, but I hope you understand that there were way worse people than you in the Bible, and God turned them into heroes.

I can't promise you'll experience the same success they did, nor the successes I've had. God's plan here on earth looks different for each of us. What I can promise is that God loves you with a burning passion that you can't even comprehend, and that as long and hard as this life may seem, an eternity in paradise awaits you in heaven.

His love overcomes your weakness. He's done the heavy lifting. He's run to you.

All you have to do is open your arms and receive Him.

> My flesh and my heart may fail, but God is the strength of my heart and my portion forever. (Psalm 73:26)

Let's finish my car story.

As it turned out, my life was not over at age sixteen. Sure, there was some pain involved, I had a ticket on my record, and repairs to the car cost around four thousand dollars. My mistake cost both my parents and me, and it could have been avoided if I had paid closer attention to the law.

But I'll never forget my parents' reaction. When they arrived at the scene, they didn't care about the car. They reassured me and showed me the very type of love of which I felt completely undeserving. I'm sure they were frustrated that my carelessness had ruined their investment and would cost them more money, but I didn't feel any resentment from them. All I remember is love and forgiveness; they knew I was hurting and that I was sorry, and they wanted to help me heal and make things right.

If two humans can extend that grace, imagine what God can do.

> Let us then with confidence draw near to the throne of grace, that we may receive mercy and find grace to help in time of need. (Hebrews 4:16)

> For by grace you have been saved through faith. And this is not your own doing; it is the gift of God. (Ephesians 2:8)

> But if it is by grace, it is no longer on the basis of works; otherwise grace would no longer be grace. (Romans 11:6)

Wherever life finds you right now, no matter how broken you feel, I pray you run to your Father. He longs so much to embrace you, and He has such wonderful things in store for you! He doesn't care how many car crashes you're in. He'll show up, throw His arm around your shoulder, and comfort you.

I sincerely thank you so much for reading this book. I humbly acknowledge that I'm not worthy of your valuable time, and none of these words are my own. Rather, they are inspired by Scripture and influenced by the Holy Spirit.

Let's close with this: God loves you. And He wants you, no matter what you've done.

If you need proof, just look at how God responds.